T0329022

CAMBRIDGE LIBRARY COLLECTION

Books of enduring scholarly value

Slavery and Abolition

The books reissued in this series include accounts of historical events and movements by eye-witnesses and contemporaries, as well as landmark studies that assembled significant source materials or developed new historiographical methods. The series includes work in social, political and military history on a wide range of periods and regions, giving modern scholars ready access to influential publications of the past.

The Anti-Slavery Cause in America and its Martyrs

Eliza Wigham (1820–99), Scots philanthropist and champion of women's rights, was raised as a Quaker, and from an early age was involved in fundraising and other support for the abolitionist cause in the United States. She published this short book in 1863, with the aim of countering pressure on the British government to support the Confederacy by describing 'the frightful reality of scenes daily and hourly acting in the United States … a complication of crimes and wrongs and cruelties, that make angels weep'. She takes the story of the American abolitionist movement from its beginnings in Philadelphia in 1775, through the founding of the American Anti-Slavery Society in 1833, to the present state of hostilities between the north and the south. Interwoven with this narrative are stories of individual hardship and cruelty that make harrowing reading, and justify the use of the term 'martyrs' in the book's title.

Cambridge University Press has long been a pioneer in the reissuing of out-of-print titles from its own backlist, producing digital reprints of books that are still sought after by scholars and students but could not be reprinted economically using traditional technology. The Cambridge Library Collection extends this activity to a wider range of books which are still of importance to researchers and professionals, either for the source material they contain, or as landmarks in the history of their academic discipline.

Drawing from the world-renowned collections in the Cambridge University Library and other partner libraries, and guided by the advice of experts in each subject area, Cambridge University Press is using state-of-the-art scanning machines in its own Printing House to capture the content of each book selected for inclusion. The files are processed to give a consistently clear, crisp image, and the books finished to the high quality standard for which the Press is recognised around the world. The latest print-on-demand technology ensures that the books will remain available indefinitely, and that orders for single or multiple copies can quickly be supplied.

The Cambridge Library Collection brings back to life books of enduring scholarly value (including out-of-copyright works originally issued by other publishers) across a wide range of disciplines in the humanities and social sciences and in science and technology.

The Anti-Slavery Cause in America and its Martyrs

ELIZA WIGHAM

CAMBRIDGE
UNIVERSITY PRESS

CAMBRIDGE
UNIVERSITY PRESS

University Printing House, Cambridge, CB2 8BS, United Kingdom

Cambridge University Press is part of the University of Cambridge.
It furthers the University's mission by disseminating knowledge in the pursuit of
education, learning and research at the highest international levels of excellence.

www.cambridge.org
Information on this title: www.cambridge.org/9781108075640

© in this compilation Cambridge University Press 2015

This edition first published 1863
This digitally printed version 2015

ISBN 978-1-108-07564-0 Paperback

THE

ANTI-SLAVERY CAUSE IN AMERICA

AND

ITS MARTYRS.

BY ELIZA WIGHAM.

" Pledging ourselves that, under the guidance and help of Almighty God, we will do all that in us lies, consistently with this declaration of our principles, to overthrow the most execrable system of slavery that has been ever witnessed upon earth; to deliver our land from its deadliest curse; to wipe out the foulest stain that rests upon our national escutcheon; and to secure to the coloured population of the United States all the rights and privileges that belong to them as men and as Americans—come what may to our persons, our interests, or our reputation—whether we live to witness the triumph of Liberty, Justice, and Humanity, or perish untimely as martyrs in this great, benevolent, and holy Cause."—*Declaration of Sentiments, signed and issued at the formation of the American Anti-Slavery Society, Dec. 6, 1833.*

LONDON:

A. W. BENNETT, 5 BISHOPSGATE STREET WITHOUT.

MDCCCLXIII.

PREFACE.

In presenting this little offering to the Anti-Slavery Cause, it is only necessary to say, that the incidents it contains have been carefully gathered from the most authentic sources, with an earnest desire to adhere strictly to truth in fact and inference, and to leave the narrative and the actors in it to speak for themselves.

It has been difficult, within prescribed limits, to make selections from the great mass of valuable Anti-Slavery literature of the last thirty years; but should any, from a perusal of these meager selections, wish to extend their information, the same deeply interesting sources from which they are taken are open to others also, and will amply repay the research by affording more intimate acquaintance with some of the finest sentiments, utterances, and actions, to be found in the history of men.

It is very important to bear in mind the character of Slavery, in order to estimate the urgency of the call which the Abolitionists felt bound to obey, " to cry aloud and spare not." It is also important to remember the intimate connexion of Slavery with the whole social, religious, and political organization of America, in order rightly to appreciate the courage of those who began to assail it—two or three against the millions.

" Then to side with Truth is noble, when we share her wretched crust,
Ere her cause bring fame and profit, and 'tis prosperous to be just;
Then it is the brave man chooses, while the coward stands aside—
Doubting in his abject spirit, till his Lord is crucified,
And the multitude make virtue of the faith they had denied."

The late Dr. Andrew Thomson, of St. George's, Edinburgh, says, " Slavery belies the doctrines—it contradicts the precepts—it resists the power—it sets at defiance the sanctions of religion—it is the tempter, and the murderer, and the tomb of virtue."

Harriet Beecher Stowe says, " Nothing of tragedy can be written, can be spoken, can be conceived, that equals the frightful reality. of scenes daily and hourly acting in the United States, beneath the shadow of American law, and the shadow of the cross of Christ;" and Miss M. Griffiths, recently a slaveholder, says, " Mrs. Stowe knows only the *echo* of the system." Mr. Thome, also a slaveholder, says, " Though I am heir to a slave inheritance, I am bold to denounce the whole system as an outrage, a complication of crimes and wrongs and cruelties, that make angels weep."

Such being the case, may all whose eyes rest on these pages be stimulated to a strong determination to do all that in them lies to guard our beloved country from any action, social or political, which may tend to ally her with a Confederacy having for its corner-stone American Slavery, the deadly enemy of the poor slave, and of Righteousness and Freedom throughout the world, and the impious rejecter and opposer of every law and attribute of Almighty God.

And now, in the earnest wish to do some little thing, however humbly, in a Cause which is that of Liberty, Humanity, Truth, and Righteousness, which, in short, is emphatically that of our Lord and Redeemer, the following pages are committed to the Public.

                                            E. W.

Edinburgh, 7th month, 1863.

CONTENTS

ANTI-SLAVERY CAUSE IN AMERICA

AND ITS MARTYRS.

~~~~~~~~~~~~~~~~

CHAPTER I.

EARLY ABOLITION MOVEMENTS.—CALL OF WM. LLOYD GARRISON;—
HIS FIRST IMPRISONMENT.—STARTING OF THE LIBERATOR.

EVERYTHING associated with America at the present
time must necessarily be of interest to British readers,
especially everything bearing on the fearful aspect of
matters prevailing in that country, and on the cause of
the fratricidal war now waging there. The war has
originated in a determination on the part of the South
to maintain, perpetuate, and, above all, to *extend* the
infamous institution of slavery; and the interests of
freedom throughout the world are affected by the success or overthrow of this manifestation of overweening
tyranny and despotism. This determination on the
part of the South has been brought to a crisis by a
growing sentiment at the North against the extension
of slavery, and whatever mixture there may be in the
motives of the North in repelling the outburst of the
South, we cannot doubt that the cause of the slave
will become more and more a prominent element in the

struggle, and that out of this state of things will come his final deliverance. Therefore, all who are interested in the cause of humanity must watch the contest with intense earnestness, fervently desiring its speedy termination, which can only be righteously effected by the emancipation of the most oppressed of the human race.

The slave in America, and the tried friends of the slave, must ever have the sympathy of the lovers of freedom in Britain, many of whose fathers suffered and died for their own civil and religious liberty, and who have themselves laboured so nobly for the abolition of British colonial slavery. Under this conviction, we venture to present a brief summary of the leading events that have marked the anti-slavery enterprise in America,—an enterprise which has enlisted in its ranks some of the most persevering and most disinterested men and women who have performed a part in the history of the world; fearlessly they endured calumny, the loss of reputation and worldly wealth, persecutions, imprisonments, death, for the sake of the despised and down-trodden slave. It is fitting that their names should be recorded in our grateful memories; and although history may not deem them worthy of a place, they may hereafter be hailed in the great day of account with the gracious words, " Inasmuch as ye have done it unto one of the least of these my brethren, ye have done it unto *Me*."

The first abolition society was formed in Philadelphia in 1775, by a few benevolent persons of different religious denominations, the majority of whom were members of the Society of Friends, to which body belonged Anthony Benezet, the most active anti-slavery worker of the period. He was the friend and corre- spondent of Granville Sharpe and the Abbé Raynal, and, in after times, of Thomas Clarkson, and many others. The child of wealthy Huguenots, who escaped from France after the revocation of the Edict of Nantes when Anthony was an infant, he inherited the love of civil and religious liberty, which in his matured phi- lanthropy he extended towards all the nations of the earth. Benjamin Lay and Ralph Sandiford preceded him in this work, but Benezet was the first effectually to call public attention to the wrongs of the negro, and to enlist the most eminent philanthropists in Eng- land and America in the struggle which eventually overthrew the slave-trade, and, as far as England's colonies were concerned, slavery itself. With the co- operation of that faithful, humble follower of his Lord and Master, John Woolman, he laboured earnestly with his brethren in religious profession, to awaken them to a just sense of the sin of slaveholding. The result of these efforts was, that in 1774 all the slaves held by " Friends" in Pennsylvania were emancipated. In other states the example was gradually followed, till, in 1787, no slave was any longer held in bondage by any member of that religious society, and slaveholding has ever since been an offence visited by disownment from their fellowship. Had this course, which was also that of the Scottish Covenanters from their first settle- ment in America, and in later years that of a very few smaller religious bodies, been faithfully pursued, we should not now have the sad spectacle, in the midst of the nineteenth century, of brother going to war against brother for the right to maintain, extend, and perpetuate the atrocious system of American slavery. If the American Church, we repeat, had been faithful in this matter, slavery would long ago have vanished under the ban of a church worthy to take the name of Him who came to preach deliverance to the captives. On the American Church, therefore, mainly rests the guilt of fostering slavery, and consequently the burden and responsibility of this war.

The anti-slavery movement, thus commenced, spread gradually, till at length chattel slavery was abolished in seven of the thirteen original states of the American Union, and the distinction between the free and the slave states took place. It is probable the system might have gradually died out altogether, had not the gins been invented, by means of which cotton wool is much more easily prepared for market, so that the cultivation of cotton began to be very profitable, the value of slaves became proportionally increased, the Southern planters kept therefore a tighter hold on their valuable *property*, and to propitiate them in order to promote their own profitable commerce with the South, the Northern merchants attempted to gloss over the iniquity of slavery, whilst the ministers and churches lent themselves to this matter; they received slaveholders to their communion, accepted their contributions for missionary and other benevolent objects, and threw the mantle of church-fellowship and sanction over the slaveholder and his deeds. Thus the progress of emancipation was arrested, the hold of

slavery on the nation grew stronger and stronger;
apathy prevailed in regard to this leprosy, which
speedily tainted the whole civil and religious society
of America; and prejudice against colour exercised its
cruel influence to keep in a degraded condition those
who, by great and heroic efforts, had freed themselves,
and were respectably striving to procure maintenance
and instruction in an honest and honourable way, and
whom, shortly afterwards, the Colonization Society
sought to banish from the country.

Things were in this state when an influence arose
which so disturbed them, that quiet on the question
of slavery has not since been known in America.
About the year 1828, the soul of William Lloyd Garrison was suddenly touched by the horrors of slavery,
and, fired by the determination to devote his life to its
overthrow, he thenceforth became the pioneer in a
fresh crusade against this fearful iniquity. This remarkable man was born on the 10th of December,
1805. His father was a sea captain, but it was from
his mother he inherited the adherence to principle
and determination of character which so remarkably
distinguish him. Her name was Fanny Lloyd; she
was very beautiful and very gay, but in her youth
she was arrested in the midst of frivolity by convictions of sin, which came to her one day when,
with foolish companions, for a frolic, she attended a
meeting of Baptists, then a despised and persecuted
sect. The words she that day heard became as nails
fastened in a sure place; she received impressions
which never deserted her. Before long, these con-

victions led her to renounce her gay associates and the pleasures of the world, and to unite with the despised Baptists, although her doing so involved expulsion from her father's house, and the contempt of all her former acquaintances. Persecution only strengthened her religious faith, which supported her through the many and sore trials she was called to bear. Left by her husband with five young children, she struggled to maintain them, and while doing so, by acting in the capacity of sick-nurse at Baltimore, she continued to be the guide of her son William, then six hundred miles off at Boston. William, after receiving a humble education, and having tried two different trades, had that of printer suggested to him by a kind friend who had been as a father to him— Deacon Ezekiel Bartlett. Here the young Garrison, then thirteen years of age, was quite in his element; he had found a vocation which was so much to his taste, that he has been heard to say that the handling of types was perfectly delightful to him, and his editorial articles in after days were frequently transferred immediately to the types, without the intermediate process of pen and ink. At the age of sixteen, he made his first attempt at authorship, in the shape of anonymous letters to the editor of the paper which employed him as a printer. These letters were so good, that it was long before his master detected their author in his apprentice. When he did so, instead of resenting the liberty that had been taken, he associated young Garrison with him in the editorship of the paper till the expiry of his apprenticeship. After this period he had many changes of circumstances, in one of which he was editor of a paper devoted to *total abstinence*, called the *National Philanthropist*, which was the first paper ever issued to promulgate this cause. Through all these changes his character was ripening for the career which was shortly to open before him.

A philanthropist named Benjamin Lundy had started, in Baltimore, the first journal in America devoted to the defence of the negro's rights; it was called the *Genius of Universal Emancipation*. Garrison read this paper, his heart was aroused at once to see a new purpose and aim of his existence, and he vowed henceforth to consecrate his life, as far as possible, to the deliverance of his enslaved fellow-countrymen. About this time he was employed at Bennington, in the state of Vermont, as editor to a paper, called *The Spirit of the Times*, which was started mainly to promote the election to Congress of John Quincy Adams, —but the editor likewise advocated temperance, peace, moral reforms, and the abolition of slavery in its columns; and he also took measures to procure from the state a petition against slavery, which was very numerously signed. When these efforts became known to Benjamin Lundy, he visited this talented and energetic co-worker, and at once offered him a partnership in his paper, entreating him to help in this great work; and as a ready vent for the hatred of slavery which burned within him, Garrison promptly consented.

It was not very long before a great difference appeared between these two partners. Although they

were equally earnest for the abolition of slavery,
Lundy's cautious mind tended towards *gradual* emancipation, while Garrison very soon saw, both by reason
and reflection, that *immediate* and unconditional
emancipation was the only remedy and atonement for
the guilt of slavery.

It was about the year 1824 that Elizabeth Heyrick,
an Englishwoman, published a pamphlet, entitled
" Immediate not Gradual Emancipation;" while in
Scotland it was suggested by Dr. Andrew Thomson of
Edinburgh that gradualism was merely an intermin-
able lengthening out of the sufferings of the slave, and
they gave the watchword of IMMEDIATE EMANCIPATION
under which the anti-slavery hosts of Britain marched
on to victory; and it was the same light, almost at
the same time, which had dawned on the young printer
in Maryland. Those who remember the struggle for
abolition in our own colonies will recollect the outcry
which greeted that noble watchword given forth in the
old Assembly Rooms of Edinburgh—the slaveholders
felt their death-thrust had been sent forth, and with
bitter malignity they assailed the friends of the slave.
So it was with young Garrison, but the hatred was intensified a hundredfold by the blow being given in the
very face of a *present* enemy.   Benjamin Lundy,
although not agreeing fully with the ardent views of
his young partner, allowed him to enunciate them,
and immediately the paper was denounced as fanatical and dangerous. Lundy's previous moderation
was of no avail, the subscribers fell off on all hands,
and the slaveholders determined to crush the paper

under the forms of law. The opportunity to do this occurred in the spring of 1830. A merchant of New-buryport, named Todd, whom Garrison had known from infancy, sent one of his ships laden with slaves to the Southern market. The circumstance of a New Englandman being engaged in this iniquitous trade so filled with indignation the breast of Garrison, that he denounced the horrible traffic in the terms it merited. Mr. Todd was exasperated, and aided by the Southern slaveholders, he brought an action for libel against Garrison; the latter proved at the court, from customhouse books, &c., that the number of slaves actually conveyed by the vessel exceeded that stated in the paper, and that his charges against Mr. Todd were truth and no libel. But in vain, the judge before whom he was tried, one Nicholas Brice, a notoriously pro-slavery man, was extremely anxious to annihilate Garrison and his paper; the jury was packed, and so it was easy to convict the accused of libel. He was sentenced to pay a fine which was far beyond his means, and was therefore sent to prison, to a cell which had just been vacated by a murderer. Here he continued the same undaunted friend of liberty; he employed his time in writing a sketch of his mock trial, which was afterwards printed and widely circulated, exciting in many minds intense indignation against the administrators, and sympathy with the victim, of such unrighteous judgment.

He also employed many hours in inscribing on the walls of his prison the breathings of his free spirit. Two of these inscriptions we may be allowed to reproduce. The first appears to be addressed to some possible successor in his undeserved imprisonment:—

I.

Prisoner, within those massive walls close pent,
   Guiltless of horrid crime or trivial wrong,
Bear nobly up against thy punishment,
   And in thy innocence be great and strong.
Perchance thy fault was love to all mankind;
   Thou didst oppose some vile oppressive end,
Or strive all human fetters to unbind;
   Or wouldst not bear the implements of war;
What then? Dost thou so soon repent the deed?
   A martyr's crown is richer than a king's!
Think it an honour with thy Lord to bleed,
   And glory, midst intensest sufferings!
Though beaten, imprison'd, put to open shame,
Time shall embalm and magnify thy name.

II.

THE FREEDOM OF THE MIND.

High walls and huge the body may confine,
   And iron grates obstruct the prisoner's gaze,
And iron bolts may baffle his design,
   And vigilant keepers watch his devious ways;
Yet scorns the immortal mind this base control;
   No chain can bind it and no cell enclose;
Swifter than light, it flies from pole to pole,
   And in a flash from earth to heaven it goes!
It leaps from mount to mount, from vale to vale;
   It wanders, plucking honeyed fruits and flowers;
It visits home, to hear the fireside tale,
   Or in sweet converse pass the joyous hours;
'Tis up before the sun, roaming afar,
   And in its watches wearies every star!

After he had been in prison upwards of a month, he was liberated by the kindness of Arthur Tappan, a wealthy merchant of New York, personally a stranger, but who had become acquainted with Garrison's character through his writings. This gentleman, who afterwards became honourably known in the cause, forwarded the amount of the fine, and the champion of emancipation was again free. New difficulties, however, were found to beset his path. The weekly paper in which he was associated with Lundy could not be sustained; he therefore retired, leaving it to be conducted monthly by its original proprietor, who continued as long as he lived to be a zealous friend of the slave, although not so prominent as his youthful ally. Two sonnets were penned by Garrison in memory of Lundy, in one of which he says:—

> Of *Freedom's* friends the truest of the true
> Wast thou, as all her deadly foes well knew;
> For bravely her good cause thou didst maintain.
> No threats could move, no perils could appal,
>   No bribes seduce thee in thy high career.
> O, many a fettered slave shall mourn thy fall,
>   And many a ransomed one let drop the tear;
> A nation wakened by the trumpet call—
>   The world itself—thy memory shall revere!

Still the strong voice within urged Garrison to plead for outraged humanity. His poverty, his recent release from prison, and other circumstances, might have induced him to remain in obscurity, but he *could not.* He therefore went north, and attempted to obtain a hearing for his cause in Boston, but for a long time in vain; and it was not until after he had announced his intention to lecture on Boston Common that a hall was offered him, in which to plead for the dumb.

Conviction was produced by these lectures on many

minds, but very few men of wealth and influence were
disposed to aid him.   The friends of the Colonization
Society,—the fallacies and covert iniquity of which he
had thought it right to expose,—were his enemies, and
the press was generally opposed to him.   The papers
which had advocated his principles had suffered, and
none would now open their columns to his appeals.
In this state of matters, the bold thought seized him
of starting a journal of his own.   His friends shook
their heads at the fanatical rashness.   How could a
man standing alone, without a penny, start, and still
less sustain, a newspaper ?

Thanks, however, to good old Ezekiel Bartlett, he
knew how to print, and, besides this, he had a friend,
named Isaac Knapp, who was also a printer ; with him
he took counsel, and the result was, that though very
poor, with not even sixpence of capital between them,
they determined to *work*.   They could *work*.   There
was a third friend, a foreman in a printing establishment, and to him they offered their services, and
engaged with him as journeymen, on condition that
their labour should cover the expenses of this important
paper, which was already called the *Liberator*.

On the 1st January, 1831, the first number was
published.   In the beginning, only a few coloured people were its supporters; but it was not many weeks
before its bold proprietors were in a condition to buy
some second-hand type and an old press, which they
set up in a small upper room.   For several years the
Liberator was issued from this small upper room,
which, during a considerable portion of that time,

served its proprietors for printing-office, bed-room, and counting-house, these noble, self-denying partners living in the most simple manner. Their diet was principally bread and water. When the paper sold particularly well, as Knapp afterwards remarked, they treated themselves to a bowl of milk. Thus, as Lowell says,—

" In a small chamber, friendless and unseen,
    Toiled o'er his types one poor, unlearned young man;
The place was dark, unfurnitured, and mean,
    Yet there the freedom of a race began.

" Help came, but slowly; surely no man yet
    Put lever to the heavy world with less.
What need of help? He knew how types were set—
    He had a dauntless spirit and a press."

A dauntless spirit truly, as the opening address to the public proved. " I am aware (he says) that many object to the severity of my language; but is there not cause for severity? I *will* be as harsh as Truth, and as uncompromising as Justice. I am in earnest. I will not equivocate, I will not excuse, I will not retreat a single inch; AND I WILL BE HEARD. The apathy of the people is enough to make every statue leap from its pedestal, and to hasten the resurrection of the dead. I desire to thank God that he enables me to disregard the fear of man, and to speak His truth in its simplicity and power." One year after the establishment of the *Liberator*, the first meeting of the American Anti-Slavery Society was held. It consisted of about a dozen members. The formation of this society was the signal for scattering much seed abroad, and many

adherents joined it. But in proportion to its progress was the bitter hostility of the slaveholders,
and their determination to oppose the new doctrine
which threatened to overthrow their darling system of
iniquity.

At the close of 1834 it was found that the auxiliary
anti-slavery societies had increased to two hundred;
and the Executive Committee of the parent society,·
in their report to their constituents, felt bound to
" thank God and take courage."

About this time Garrison visited England, to unmask
the true character of the Colonization Society, which
he clearly perceived was a scheme to get rid of *free
people of colour*, lest slave property should be endangered. In England he met with the leaders of the
anti-slavery enterprise, who cordially received and
highly appreciated him. He had several friendly and
interesting interviews with Wilberforce shortly before
his death, and had the melancholy privilege of attend-
ing the funeral of that great man in Westminster
Abbey.

CHAPTER II.

MARIA WESTON CHAPMAN AND THE WOMEN OF THE ANTI-SLAVERY
CAUSE.—THE BOSTON MOB OF 21ST OCTOBER, 1835.—PRUDENCE
CRANDALL.—HEROISM REGARDLESS OF LIFE.—LYDIA MARIA CHILD.
—PERSECUTIONS OF THE COLOURED PEOPLE.—JAMES G. BIRNEY.—
LANE SEMINARY.—HEROIC DETERMINATION AND SELF-SACRIFICE
OF THE STUDENTS.—FOUNDATION OF OBERLIN COLLEGE.—AMOS
DRESSER.

THE hatred against Garrison in the United States
intensified from day to day. In 1829, a coloured man
named Walker, who issued an appeal to the coloured
people to rise and assert their rights, was found murdered at his own door. Garrison was threatened with
the fate of Walker; he was told that " he would not
be permitted to live long;" that " he would be taken
away, and that no man would be the wiser for it."
His answer to this was characteristic of his spirit:—
" Will you aim at no higher victims than Arthur
Tappan, George Thompson,* and William Lloyd Garrison? Who and what are they? Three drops from
a boundless ocean—three rays from a noon-day sun—
three particles of dust floating in a limitless atmosphere
—nothing abstracted from infinite fulness! Should

* In 1834 Geo. Thompson, then at the height of his popularity
in Great Britain, having been the most powerful instrument in
obtaining West Indian emancipation, was deputed by the anti-
slavery societies of Edinburgh and Glasgow to carry a message of sympathy to the faithful abolitionists of America, and to
aid their work. He, taking his life in his hand, cheerfully threw
in his lot with theirs. The hostility against him had additional
bitterness from the fact that he was a foreigner, and he very
nearly fell a sacrifice to this hostility.

you succeed in destroying them, the mighty difficulty
still remains."

And Garrison was not alone in labour or in suffering; the insults, privations, and anxieties, which the
abolitionists had to endure, cannot be estimated. Wives
sitting quietly at home often received intimation of
personal violence intended to their husbands; children
came home, crying and in distress from the cruel
taunts and outrages of their companions, while their
fathers had to suffer in those dearest to them, as well
as in their own persons. It was no outward strength
that sustained them in those days of trial.

In 1835 occurred the memorable mob, which must
ever form a disgraceful page of the history of Boston.
For some time there had existed in Boston a Ladies'
Anti-Slavery Society. It was composed, as may well
be believed, of real heroines; for at that time, to em-
brace the cause of the slave was to risk the loss of
reputation, and even life. These women were stead-
fast to what they believed their duty to God and
man. As one of their earliest reports says, " There
is an exceeding great reward in faithful obedience;—
the clearer and deeper views of duty it gives, the
greater love of God and man, the deliverance from
fear and constraint, the less apprehension of suffering;
' the more freedom to die.' Enjoying these, may we
never look for any reward less spiritual and enduring.
We pray, for the sake of the oppressed, that God will
aid us to banish from our hearts every vestige of selfishness; for in proportion to our disinterestedness,
will be our moral power for their deliverance."

Such was the temper of the ladies who, on the 21st of October 1835, called a meeting of their own society, and attempted to hold it. Thirty succeeded in entering the hall, the rest were held back by a mob of thousands of " gentlemen of property and standing." Maria Weston Chapman, the leader of the noble band, had been warned of the danger to their lives which they incurred by holding a meeting. She had herself gone round quietly to carry the warning from house to house. Among those she visited was an artizan's wife, who was sweeping out her two rooms as Mrs. Chapman entered. On being told of the danger, in order that she might stay away if she thought proper, she leaned on her broom a few minutes, and then said, " I have often wished and asked that I might be able to do something for the poor slave, and it seems to me that this is the very time and the very way. You shall see me at the meeting, and I will keep a prayerful mind, as I am about my work till then."

When the ladies gathered in the hall, their president, Mary Parker, read a portion of the Bible with dignity and solemnity, and then engaged in fervent prayer to God for protection and succour, and for forgiveness of enemies. The clear tones of her voice were heard above the hootings and yellings of the mob, and even some of the crowd were overawed by the sublime spectacle of thirty women sitting unmoved in the midst of such fearful circumstances. The mayor came, and, on the plea that it was out of his power to control the mob, as Mrs. Chapman quietly suggested his doing, he

C

entreated the ladies to disperse. To this they calmly consented, Mrs. Chapman advising her companions to go home and quietly resume their domestic occupations. Mr. Garrison, who came to the meeting to escort his young wife, then near to her confinement, was seen by the mob, who assailed him violently with cries of " Lynch him ! Lynch him !" One of his friends rushed forward armed in his defence. " My dear brother," said this Christian hero, " you know not what spirit you are of. This is the trial of our faith. Shall we give blow for blow, and draw sword against sword ? God forbid ! If my life be taken, the cause of emancipation will not suffer. God reigns, and his omnipotence will at length be victorious." The mob hurried him to a window with the intention of hurling him from it, but an exclamation from some one of " Do not let us kill him outright," deterred them; so he was spared. A rope was then tied round his body, to enable the furious crowd the better to drag him to the tar-kettle. His hat was knocked from his head, and brick-bats were raining in all directions. At this juncture his young wife, who knew him to be in the hands of the mob, stepped, in the excitement of the moment, from a window to the roof of a shed, and saw her husband in this extreme danger. And what were the only words that escaped from the white lips of this gentle, loving woman ? " I *think* my husband will not deny his principles. I AM SURE my husband will not deny his principles."

He was dragged onwards by the infuriated rabble. At one time a diversion in his favour was caused by

the cry, " He is an American; he shall not be hurt."
But again the multitude rushed upon him; his clothes
were torn from him, and nothing but his life, it seemed,
would satisfy his ferocious assailants. Eye-witnesses
have asserted that during this time nothing could ex-
ceed the calm stedfast courage of this brave man. His
countenance was as unruffled as that of an apostolic
martyr, and there was something beautiful in its
serenity. He himself declared that " it seemed to him
a blessed privilege to suffer thus in the cause of Christ.
Death did not present a repulsive feature. The pro-
mises of God sustained his soul, so that he was not
only devoid of fear, but ready to sing aloud for joy!"
Through the mercy of God his life was spared, and he
was lodged for safety in prison, where with a good
conscience he sat down in peace, and as usual proceeded to make inscriptions on the walls, one of which
runs thus :—

" William Lloyd Garrison was put into this cell on Wednesday
afternoon, Oct. 21st, 1835, to save him from the violence of a
respectable and influential mob, who sought to destroy him for
preaching the abominable and dangerous doctrine that all men
are equal, and that all oppression is odious in the sight of God."

Next day he was released, but, at the earnest en-
treaties of the city authorities, he left Boston for a
little time.

In the order of time, we ought before this period to
have mentioned the introduction to the cause and its
martyrdom of Miss Prudence Crandall. On the 2nd of
March, 1833, she advertised that she would receive
into her female boarding-school " young ladies and
c c

little misses of colour," giving references to a long list of gentlemen of great respectability. The reason of this announcement was that she had lately admitted a little girl of light colour among her white pupils, and had subsequently admitted a second, thereby offending the parents of her white pupils, who threatened to withdraw their children if any more were introduced into the school of a darker complexion. Miss Crandall nobly resolved to continue to receive coloured children, and to let the whites go if they would. A town meeting was called on the appearance of the advertisement, and the school was denounced in violent terms. Miss Crandall silently prosecuted her plan. The state legislature was petitioned, and a law was obtained in May, making it a penal offence to establish any school for the instruction of coloured persons not inhabitants of the state, or to instruct, board, or harbour such entering the state for educational purposes. As this law was clearly unconstitutional, Miss Crandall took no notice of it, but went on with her school. She was accordingly arrested and carried before a justice of the peace, and the next spectacle seen in the village of Canterbury was Miss Crandall going to jail. She was bailed out next day, and her trial set aside, as the jury could not agree. She was again and again prosecuted, and at length convicted. She then appealed to a higher court, and struggled on through a long prosecution, but was at length compelled to yield from the lives of her pupils being in danger. Her fences were pulled down, her wells filled up, the traders in the place refused to deal with her, and she was obliged to purchase necessaries from a great distance; she and her pupils were refused admission to the churches, her windows were repeatedly broken in the night, and at length the attacks on her house became so alarming, and the menaces to her pupils so violent, that the parents were compelled to hide their children in their houses, and Miss Crandall retired from the place. Her conduct was to the last degree meek and quiet throughout, and her courage was worthy of the cause and of the Master she served.

By this year, 1834, the abolition cause was aided by many periodicals, and several fearless individuals published books in behalf of the slave. Among these was Mrs. Child, whose works were exceedingly popular in America before she wrote her " Appeal on behalf of that class of Americans called Africans;" but afterwards the sale of her valuable household volumes declined, and she suffered in estate and reputation for venturing to plead for the oppressed. The recognition of people of colour as brethren and sisters, in the most incidental way of ordinary civility, was the signal for the loss of caste, and for reproach and scorn from former associates. But the abolitionists had their reward in seeing the stimulus given to these hitherto depressed people, who were now determined to band together for mutual improvement. The schools had been closed against them, the churches sent them to separate lofts, where, whatever might be their refinement and respectability, they were obliged to worship apart from the white congregation, and everywhere they were shut out from social privileges. But now hope arose, and

they determined to secure education for themselves
and their children, that they might be fitted to assert
their manhood and to labour for their race. The
struggle was long and earnest, and the sufferings
through which they and their faithful friends passed
in seeking to secure their rights, were very severe.

It was in 1834 that the fury of the mob on this subject reached its height. In Philadelphia forty-four
houses and two churches belonging to people of colour
were besieged; some few were greatly damaged, and
the rest sacked and destroyed. In New York, on
the 4th of July, the anniversary of the declaration
of independence, the house of Mr. Lewis Tappan was
sacked, and the furniture burned in the street; the
African school-house in Orange Street, and twelve
adjacent houses, chiefly belonging to people of colour,
were destroyed; St. Philip's Church was sacked, and
several others were much damaged. And all this time,
while the abolitionists were suffering the loss of property
and the absence of security for life and limb, they were
charged as being the cause of the tumult, and endured
the most bitter and scurrilous vituperations of the
press, and the contempt of those in high places. But
they had sources of strength which such assaults could
not reach, and accepting these persecutions as evidence
that their attacks on slavery were not unfelt, they
hoped and laboured on. They were not without encou-
ragement from a very unexpected quarter. From the
hotbed of Slavery where the negro toils and dies before
his time from suffering and oppression, from Alabama
itself, there arose a mighty auxiliary, in James G. Bir-

ney, a slaveholder, a man of rank and wealth and political influence, who suddenly declared himself an abolitionist. He was solicitor-general of the state, and was
likely to receive further promotion. But he was an
honest man, true to the convictions that had entered
his soul. He removed from Alabama, emancipated and
settled all his slaves, and started a newspaper in Cincinnati; where, notwithstanding fearful attempts on
his life and liberty, he stood his ground and established freedom of speech and of the press. It was
Mr. Birney who, in after days of advanced light, wrote
that remarkable essay, " The American Churches the
Bulwark of American Slavery," a title the truth of
which was proved by the contents of the pamphlet,
and which has received mournful confirmation every
year since it was written.

In 1834 also arose combinations of young men with
souls fired for this great and chivalrous contest against
oppression. The most remarkable accession of this
kind emanated from Lane Seminary, Cincinnati, a
Presbyterian college of high standing, of which the late
Dr. Beecher was president. The students, most of them
above twenty-one years of age, were in the habit of
discussing the great questions of the day; as they
themselves say in their statement of reasons for their
conduct afterwards put forth, " The circumstances of
our matriculation were peculiarly impressive. We
were connected with an institution freighted with the
spiritual interests of the West. . . . Our probable influence over succeeding classes was also matter of
deep solicitude. . . . We aimed, therefore, to make

such a disposal of our influence as would contribute
to place Lane Seminary upon high moral ground,
and thus greatly elevate the standard and augment
the resources of ministerial efficiency. As a primary
step, we were led to adopt this principle, That *free
discussion with corresponding effort is a* DUTY, *and
of course a* RIGHT. We proceeded upon this principle, without molestation in our studies, at our reci-
tations and lectures. We applied it to missions at
home and abroad, and we *acted* immediately through
liberal contributions. We took up temperance. Discussion was needless; duty was plain, and we *acted.*
With the Sunday-school cause we proceeded in like
manner. Next moral reform came up; we examined
it in a series of adjourned meetings, light was elicited,
principles were fixed, and *action* followed. With the
same spirit of free inquiry we discussed the question of
slavery. We prayed much, heard facts, weighed arguments, kept our temper, and after the most patient
pondering, in which we were sustained by the spirit of
sympathy, not of anger, we decided that slavery was a
sin, and, as such, ought to be immediately renounced.
In this case, too, we *acted.*"

The students began to employ *their leisure hours* in
promoting Sunday-schools and other means of instruction among the free coloured population of Cincinnati.
Several of the students belonged to slaveholding families; and, as Ohio borders on two slave states, the
institution looked for its resources to this part of its
neighbourhood. And so, although every other subject
was allowed to be freely discussed, this of slavery was

forbidden as dangerous. The faculty forbade association and discussion on this question, and eventually conferred irresponsible power of expulsion on the executive committee. Thus the students felt that the whole right of free inquiry was banished, and that there was nothing left for the conscientious but to withdraw. Of the theological students, only two out of forty returned the next term; and of the classical, only five out of sixty.

Throughout the whole affair the demeanour of the students was most respectful. The president's testimony, in writing at the time, was, " The students are a set of noble men, whom I would not at a venture change for any others." The faculty gave repeated assurance that their conduct was without exception respectful and orderly, and on the withdrawal of the body they granted to each certificates of standing. These young men soberly and sadly left the seminary where they had enjoyed the acquisition of useful instruction, but they left with the solemn conviction of duty, and a full knowledge of the difficulties that were before them. Many of them were sons and brothers of slaveholders, and their lives would have been endangered by an attempt to return to their homes. Their resources were likewise cut off; and under these circumstances it may be understood that nothing but a high sense of duty could have led the " Lane Seminary boys " to the course which they adopted. By their firm decided movement a great impetus was given to the cause of freedom of thought in the West; and although the venerable president of Lane Seminary then had his

vision clouded by sympathy with the colonization
movement, his sons are not unknown to the anti-
slavery ranks, and his daughter is the celebrated
authoress of " Uncle Tom's Cabin."

Forty of the expelled students at once took steps to
found an institution where freedom of thought and
speech might be secure, and where students of all conditions in life, every theological opinion and every
colour, should be received and educated. They repaired to the forest, and set to work to clear a tract
of land in the north-east of Ohio. The first building
raised for a shelter was made of slabs—pieces of rough
wood laid one upon the other. They toiled through
the winter of 1834-35, and thus, without endowment,
and with very little pecuniary help, commenced the
college of OBERLIN—an institution which has given
many missionaries to the world, and a high tone of
principle to all connected with it. Of course, the first
difficulties of the founders were very great, but their
good fame soon spread abroad. Learned men, of noble,
disinterested character, offered themselves as teachers
to these interesting pupils; they threw off their coats
and toiled in the forest for several hours of each day,
and gave lectures during the rest. Young men and
women flocked to Oberlin to beg such instruction as
would fit them for teachers of the coloured people.
When told that there were no funds and no means of
accommodation, their answer was, " We will provide
for ourselves if you will let us stay." The building
went vigorously on till a good brick house was erected,
containing ninety-two rooms. The young men were

taught by a practical farmer, and the young women superintended the dairy, the house, and the clothes; and yet all found time to acquire such learning as would fit them to become teachers in turn.

The abstemious living of the household, professors included, was admirable; the pressure of numbers and scarcity of money compelled them to give up the use of animal food, then of tea and coffee (fermented liquors had been excluded from the first), and at last they lived on garden produce and milk; and a vigorous, healthy household they were. When the clothing was shabby, the best garments were lent to those who had to go abroad on business. One student laid down for the institution all the money he had in the world. But disinterested benefactions were not confined to the inmates of Oberlin; one farmer drove over a cow from a great distance, the only gift he had in the world to bestow; another, who lived eleven miles off, offered to accommodate the new comers who could not be received into the establishment; he boarded and lodged *seventy* for a year and a half. His wife fell a sacrifice to the toil and care thus imposed on her, but she died with perfect willingness in such a service, into which she went heart and hand with her husband. Another settler accommodated thirty students with their professor for the same length of time. Other neighbours gave what they could; and so, in spite of the pressure of the times, Oberlin stood its ground. It still stands, and it will probably be recollected that, so lately as the year 1858, its principles of liberty were severely put to the test. A poor fugitive slave, in the neigh-

bouring fields, was decoyed away and almost kidnapped
back to slavery; the students and others became aware
of the outrage, rushed to the rescue, and succeeded in
delivering the poor man and sending him off to Canada.
For this action twenty citizens, including a professor,
ministers, students, and teachers, were sent to jail,
imprisoned, and severely fined. The undaunted spirit
of Oberlin, to trust in God to sustain the right, upheld
them; and some of their utterances from the prison
were such as deserve to be recorded among the words
of martyrs and heroes.

But, between the two dates at which we have been
glancing in the history of Oberlin, many incidents
occurred bearing reference to it, a few of which should
be mentioned here. During the annual three months'
vacation, the students dispersed themselves through
the land to preach and to teach as they found opportunity. Some visited Canada, to cheer and instruct
the poor fugitives from slavery there; others travelled
up and down the states, trying to increase the abolition feeling; and wherever they went, the hearts
of the poor coloured people were strengthened, and
their minds stimulated to hold up their heads in
hope, and seek to elevate themselves to higher positions
in social and intellectual life.

In the month of July, 1835, one of the students,
Amos Dresser, travelled southwards from Cincinnati,
for the purpose of selling Bibles and a few other books,
to raise a little money to assist in his education. At
Nashville, Tennessee, he was arrested on suspicion of
being an abolition agent—a groundless charge, as he

had neither spoken to slaves nor distributed books among free people of colour. He was brought before a committee of vigilance, consisting of sixty-two of the principal citizens, of whom seven were elders of the Presbyterian Church. His trunk was examined, and in it were found three anti-slavery volumes, put in for his own reading, and a few abolition newspapers used as stuffing to prevent the books rubbing against each other; his private journal and letters were also examined, but the mayor had difficulty in deciphering them: he however put them down, observing that they were " evidently very hostile to slavery." As Amos Dresser had not anticipated any very serious issue to his trial, he was a good deal horrified on learning that his judges were debating whether his sentence should be thirty-nine lashes or a hundred (the latter number is considered fatal), or death by hanging. All the time the committee agreed that he had broken no law, but asserted the necessity of making *law for the occasion*, to protect slavery against attacks from opinion. Dresser was found guilty of three things : of belonging to an abolition society in another state, of having books of an anti-slavery tendency in his possession, and of being believed to have circulated some of these in his travels. He was sentenced to the *moderate* penalty of receiving twenty lashes in the market-place; and there, by torch-light, just as the chimes were ushering in the Sabbath morning, this brutal punishment was inflicted. Fearlessly he bore the suffering, but he uttered an exclamation of thanksgiving at the close, which was rudely overborne by oaths and

cries of " Stop his praying." Some kind stranger
drew him into his house, washed his wounds and
dressed them, and sent him on his way disguised. He
left the place on foot early in the morning, and no
redress was ever made him, neither were his books or
clothes ever returned. Surely no human strength sustained this young man in his trial, and enabled him to
stand firm to his principles then and in after times.
Amos Dresser was in this country some years ago, and
his gentle aspect and unassuming demeanour were
convincing proof that it was not in himself, but in a
higher power, that his strength lay.

CHAPTER III.

ANGELINA AND SARAH GRIMKE. — RESCUE OF TWO KIDNAPPED
WOMEN.—MASSACHUSETTS SOIL DECLARED FREE.—CONVENTION OF
ANTI-SLAVERY WOMEN.—BURNING OF PENNSYLVANIA HALL BY
THE MOB.—MARTYRDOM OF LOVEJOY.

ABOUT this time Edward Everett, then governor of
Massachusetts, had given advice that any abolitionist
demanded by the South should be " delivered up to
Southern law," which was well known to mean " delivered up to certain death," and a price was actually
set on the heads of a few distinguished abolitionists,
by the legislatures of some of the Southern States, and
they walked on their daily line of duty not knowing
but that the night might witness their dwellings in
flames, their homes invaded, and themselves hurried
off to Southern mercy.

We have alluded to the position which women were
called on to maintain in this great struggle for the
freedom of millions of their brethren and sisters held
in bondage. We must now briefly allude to two
sisters who were eminent in the moral warfare of
that day. Angelina E. and Sarah Grimké were
Quaker ladies of South Carolina, sisters of the Hon.
Thos. S. Grimké, a slaveholder, yet a gentleman who,
in point of scholarship, was one of the greatest orna-
ments of the United States, and as such was univer-
sally honoured. At his death they became heirs to his
estates. They strove, by every means in their power,
to ameliorate the condition of the slaves they had in-

herited. In defiance of the laws, they attempted to educate them. But soon finding that there is no infusing into slavery the benefits of freedom, they surrendered their worldly interests at the call of conscience. They freed their slaves, enabled them to provide for themselves in a free state, and retired to Philadelphia to live on the remains of their former opulence. But the same Divine call disturbed their quiet seclusion, and induced them to come forward with the stores of evidences from their experience of the details and workings of slavery, which they were so well qualified to give; while a peculiar adaptation for speaking made it easy for them to state to larger audiences these facts, and to present the appeals founded on them. In this way they rendered essential service to the cause. A few extracts from a letter of Angelina Grimké will show something of the spirit of these admirable women. Alluding to the Boston mobs, and her anxieties in regard to her friends there, and referring to mobs being frequently the first agents in religious persecutions, whose action was generally followed by the enactment of oppressive laws, she adds:—" Let us then be prepared for the enactment of laws, even in our free states, against abolitionists. And how ardently has the prayer been breathed, that God would prepare us for all he is preparing for us !

" My mind has been especially turned to those who are standing in the fore-front of the battle, and the prayer has gone up for their preservation,—not the preservation of their lives, but the preservation of their minds in humility and patience, faith, hope, and charity,—that charity which is the bond of perfectness. If persecution is the means which God has ordained for the accomplishment of this great end, emancipation, then, in dependence upon him for strength to bear it, I feel as if I could say, let it come; for it is my deep, solemn, deliberate conviction, that this is a cause worth dying for.

" At one time I thought this system would be over-thrown in blood with the confused noise of the warrior; but a hope gleams across my mind that *our* blood will be spilt instead of the slaveholders; our lives will be taken and theirs spared. I say a hope, for of all things I desire to be spared the anguish of seeing our beloved country desolated with the horrors of a servile war."

This lady was married in 1838 to Theodore D. Weld, one of the forty seceders from Lane Seminary. The sisters still continued to live together. They devoted their time, talents, and property to the cause. Their mode of living was of the simplest description, and the little family were thus enabled to save, for the service of the oppressed, all that might have been spent on superfluities.

Very different was the tone of another slaveholder of South Carolina, General M'Duffie, governor of the state, whose message in 1835 contained, among others, the following passages, which we give as illustrative of the arguments against which the abolitionists had to contend :—

" No human institution, in my opinion, is more manifestly consistent with the will of God than domes-tic slavery. . . .

D

" So deep is my conviction on this subject, that if I were doomed to die immediately after recording these sentiments, I would say, in all sincerity, and under the sanction of Christianity and patriotism, ' God forbid that my descendants, in the remotest generations, should live in any other than a community having the institution of domestic slavery, as it existed among the patriarchs of the primitive church, and in all the ages of antiquity !' "

One noteworthy incident of 1835 was the defence, by the abolitionists, of two poor coloured women, who had been seen making signals of distress from a brig in Boston harbour, and whom it was suspected were kidnapped. A writ of *habeas corpus* was obtained, and the women were safely lodged in jail. At the trial the anti-slavery ladies determined to be present to comfort them and aid their escape if they were *acquitted of the charge of being slaves;* for in case of acquittal on this account, the claimant very quickly brings forward some *other* criminal charge. When, therefore, Judge Shaw maintained the Bill of Rights of Massachusetts and in the midst of solemn silence arrived at the closing words, " Whence it appears that the prisoners must be discharged,"—all rose, the crowd, the council, the men of colour, and the ladies who surrounded the prisoners. A lane was quickly made, the claimant darted forth his arm to seize them, but the women were gone !

In 1836 a case of a somewhat different nature occurred, in which the abolitionists again succeeded, and established the freedom of a child brought by his master to Massachusetts as a slave, with the intent to take him back as such. Ellis Gray Loring pleaded the case before Chief-Justice Shaw; and it was henceforth decided that all slaves who should touch the soil of Massachusetts (except fugitives) should be free. This decision was followed in Connecticut; and the right of jury-trial for persons arrested as fugitive slaves was soon after established in Massachusetts, New Jersey, and Vermont.

It was not till many years later that the Fugitive Slave Law disgraced the United States, and gave a more definite form to the old clause of the Constitution, which converted the whole of the free states into hunting ground for slaves, and that the infamous Dred Scott decision decreed that " black men have no rights which white men are bound to respect."

In 1837, John Quincy Adams, an ex-president of the United States, vindicated the right of petition in the House of Representatives; a noble work, which with others of a like character will hand his name down to posterity as a benefactor of his race.

In the second week of May of that year a convention of women was held, which resolved " that it was immoral to separate persons of colour from the rest of society, especially in churches, and pledged its members to procure for this class, if possible, an equal choice of sittings with themselves; and where this was not possible, to take their seats with the despised class."*

---

* A similar course to this was adopted by a friend and countryman of our own, who resided seventeen years in New York, but who never lost his integrity and sympathy for the coloured

Another resolution was, "That whereas our fathers, husbands, and brothers have devoted themselves to the rescue of the enslaved, at the risk of ease, reputation, and life, we, their daughters, wives, and sisters, honouring their conduct, hereby pledge ourselves to uphold them by our sympathy, to share their sacrifices, and vindicate their characters."

In 1838, a second convention of women was held; and on this occasion it was that the most violent attacks were made upon them. The Legislature of Pennsylvania had been aroused to fiercer persecution of the free people of colour, and had denied them civil rights, which before had been accorded them. When, therefore, the friends of the slave began to assemble in the Quaker city, and the coloured people flocked to join them in Pennsylvania Hall, the violence and rage of

---

race in all his contact with the apologists for slavery. He had not been long attached to the Associate Reformed Congregation in New York, before he saw that, in administering the communion, four tables were served. The first three were filled by the congregation, and were quite sufficient for them, with room to spare; at the fourth were *four coloured women!* He was astonished, and made inquiry; the result of which was, that he learned the exclusion was merely on account of their colour; that these women were highly respectable. One of them was that worthy servant of her Lord, Catherine Fergusson, devoted in every good word and work, who was the counterpart of Mrs. Stowe's "Millie" in many particulars of her life and character. Our friend made many efforts to have the disgraceful anti-Christian exclusion removed. But failing in these, he declared his intention, and that of his wife, to partake of the communion *only* in company with these coloured servants of the Lord. His persistency in this course had the desired effect, and so far as the matter of communion was concerned, the reproach was removed from the congregation.

the populace knew no bounds. A yelling mob beset the doors, and fierce shouts of wrath interrupted the proceedings of the meeting; but the mild voice of Angelina Weld was heard above the uproar, and Maria W. Chapman appeared on the platform to take her stand at the post of peril. She was ill; an attack of fever rendered her almost unable to stand; but her personal beauty accorded well with the thrilling tones of her voice and the summary of duty she strove to enforce:—" Our principles teach us to avoid that spurious charity which would efface moral distinctions, and that our duty to the sinner is not to palliate, but to pardon—not to excuse, but to forgive, freely, fully, as we hope to be forgiven." The fury of the mob manifested itself in threats and insults for four days and nights, yet no action was interposed on the part of the authorities; and at last the rioters broke into the Hall, heaped the furniture and books in the centre, and burned them and the building together. Not satisfied with this sacrifice to their rage, they set fire to the Coloured Orphan Asylum, which had no more to do with abolition than any other benevolent institution in Philadelphia. After these outrages the Recorder interposed, and the city firemen came forward to protect the buildings, both public and private. The abolitionists next day collected funds and hired workmen to rebuild their hall, and issued a call for a third convention in 1839. They afterwards applied for damages, and succeeded in obtaining from the city authorities some compensation, though to a very inadequate amount.

In 1837 a very striking event occurred, which con-

cerned the freedom of the press as well as the cause of
personal liberty. This was the martyrdom of the Rev.
Elijah P. Lovejoy. He was a native of Maine, a gra-
duate of Waterville College. He settled at St. Louis,
Missouri, and attained eminence as editor of a newspaper there. He then became a clergyman, and afterwards an abolitionist. The burning at the stake, in
St. Louis, of a free coloured man named M'Intosh,
roused his indignant spirit, and he spoke out against
the atrocity of the deed. For this his press and types
were destroyed, but he established himself on the opposite side of the river, at Alton, in the free state of
Illinois. This place, however, proved not less dangerous to him; it was the resort of slave-traders
and others, who believed their interest depended on
the maintenance of slavery. For some time after his
arrival at Alton he did not feel called on to discuss the
question, but at length he saw it his duty to declare his
convictions against slavery. He called together the supporters of the paper and consulted them. They allowed
him to let his conscience have free course. He did so;
he wrote boldly for the Right, and the consequence
was that his press was three times destroyed by the
mob; but he stood firm, and his paper continued to
be the dispassionate advocate of freedom and reprover
of violence. In October he wrote to a friend in New
York a description of the murderous spirit of his assailants, who tracked his steps for weeks, and added,—
" And now, my dear brother, if you ask what are my
own feelings at a time like this, I answer,—perfectly
calm, perfectly resigned. Though in the midst of

dangers, I have a constant sense of security that keeps me alike from fear and anxiety. I read the Bible, and especially the Psalms, with a delight, a refreshing of soul, I never knew before. God has said, ' As thy day is, so shall thy strength be;' and he has made his promise good. Pray ,for me. . . . We have a few excellent brethren here in Alton. They are sincerely desirous to know their duty in this crisis, and to do it; but as yet they cannot see that duty *requires* them to maintain their cause here at all hazards. Of this be assured, the cause of truth still lives in Illinois, and will not want defenders. Whether our paper starts again will depend on our friends east, west, north, and south. So far as depends on me, it shall go forward. By the blessing of God, I shall not abandon the enterprise so long as I live, and until success has crowned it. And there are those in Illinois who join me in this resolution. And if I am to die, it cannot be in a better cause.—Yours till death or victory."

His resolution was very soon to be put to the test. A few weeks after this he was summoned before a large meeting of townsmen, and required to leave the place. He listened to what the chairman had to say, then stepped forward and delivered a most remarkable unpremeditated address—his last verbal testimony. We would gladly quote it entire, did space permit, for its thrilling words could not be read without awakening some kindred fire in the reader. However, the following extracts may suffice, to stimulate him to love the cause for which some men have dared to die:—

" I feel, Mr. Chairman, that this is the most solemn
moment of my life. I feel, I trust, in some measure
the responsibilities which at this hour I sustain to
these my fellow-citizens, to the Church of which I am
a minister, to my country, and to God. ... Mr. Chairman, I do not admit that it is the business of this
assembly to decide whether I shall or shall not publish
a newspaper in this city. I have a *right* to do it. I
know that I have a right to speak and publish my
sentiments, subject only to the laws of the land for the
abuse of that right. This right was given me by my
Maker, and is solemnly guaranteed to me by the constitution of the United States, and the laws of this
state. ... This resolution you have proposed is called
a compromise—a compromise between two parties.
Mr. Chairman, this is not so; there is but one party
here. It is simply a question whether the law shall
be enforced, or whether the mob shall be allowed, as
they now do, to continue to trample it under their
feet, by violating with impunity the rights of an innocent individual. Mr. Chairman, what have I to compromise? If freely to forgive those who have so
greatly injured me; if to pray for their temporal and
eternal happiness; if still to wish for the prosperity of
your city and state, notwithstanding all the indigni-
ties I have suffered in it; if this be the compromise
intended, then do I willingly make it! My rights
have been shamefully, wickedly outraged; this I know
and feel, and can never forget. But I can and do
freely forgive those who have done it.

" But if by a compromise is meant that I should

cease from doing that which duty requires of me, I cannot make it. And the reason is, that I fear God more than I fear man. Think not that I would lightly go contrary to public sentiment around me. The good opinion of my fellow-men is dear to me, and I would sacrifice anything but principle to obtain their good wishes. But when they ask me to surrender this, they ask for more than I can, than I dare, give. ... It is a very different question whether I shall, voluntarily and at the request of friends, yield up my post, or whether I shall forsake it at the hands of a mob. The former I am at all times ready to do, when circumstances occur to require it, as I will never put my personal wishes in competition with the cause of that Master whose minister I am. But the latter, be assured, I *never* will do. God, in his providence (so say all my brethren, and so I think), has devolved upon me the responsibility of maintaining my ground here; and, Mr. Chairman, I am determined to do it. A voice comes to me from Maine, from Massachussetts, from Connecticut, from New York, from Pennsylvania, yea, from Kentucky, from Mississippi, from Missouri, calling upon me, in the name of all that is dear in heaven and earth, to stand fast; and, by the help of God, I WILL STAND. ... You can crush me if you will; but I shall die at my post, for I cannot, and will not, forsake it. ... And do not your resolutions say that you find nothing against my private and personal character? ... You have courts and juries, they find nothing against me; and now you come together for the purpose of driving out a confessedly innocent man, for no

cause but that he dares to think and speak as his conscience and his God dictate. . . . Will conduct like this
stand the scrutiny of your country? of posterity? above
all, of the judgment day? For remember the Judge
of that day is no respecter of persons. Pause, I beseech you, and reflect. The present excitement will
soon be over; the voice of conscience will at last be
heard; and in some season of honest thought, even in
this world, as you review the scenes of this hour, you
will be compelled to say, ' He was right! he was right!'

" But you have been exhorted to be lenient and
compassionate; and, in driving me away, to affix no
unnecessary disgrace upon me. Sir, I reject all such
compassion. You cannot disgrace me. Scandal, and
falsehood, and calumny, have already done their worst.
My shoulders have borne the burden till it sits easy
upon them. You may hang me up, as the mob hung
up the individuals at Vicksburgh. You may burn me
at the stake, as they did M'Intosh at St. Louis; or you
may tar and feather me, or throw me into the Mississippi, as you have often threatened to do; but you
cannot disgrace me; I, and I alone, can disgrace myself; and the deepest of all disgrace would be at a time
like this, to deny my Master by forsaking his cause
He died for me! I were most unworthy to bear His
name, should I refuse, if need be, to die for Him!

" Again, you have been told that I have a family
dependent on me; and this has been given as a reason
why I should be driven off as gently as possible. It
is true, Mr. Chairman, I am a husband and a father;
and this it is that adds the bitterest ingredient to the

cup of sorrow I am called to drink. I know, sir, that, in this contest, I stake not my life only, but that of others also. I do not expect that my wife will ever recover the shock received in the awful scenes through which she was called to pass at St. Charles. And how was it the other night on my return to my house? I found her driven to the garret, through fear of the mob that were prowling round the house; and scarcely had I entered it, ere my windows were broken in by the brick-bats of the mob, and she so alarmed, that it was impossible for her to sleep or rest that night. I am hunted as a partridge upon the mountains; I am pursued as a felon through your streets; and to the guardian power of the law I look in vain for that protection against violence which even the vilest criminal may claim.

" Yet think not that I am unhappy. Think not that I regret the choice that I have made. While all around me is tumult and violence, all is peace within. An approving conscience and the rewarding smile of God is a full recompense for all that I forego and all that I endure. Yes, sir, I enjoy a peace which nothing can destroy. I sleep sweetly and undisturbed, except when awakened by the brick-bats of the mob.

" No, sir, I am not unhappy. I have counted the cost, and stand prepared freely to offer up my all in the service of God. Yes, sir, I am fully aware of all the sacrifice I make, in here pledging myself to continue this contest to the last. (Forgive these tears, I had not intended to shed them; and they flow not for myself, but others.) But I am commanded to forsake

father and mother, and wife and child, for Jesus' sake;
and, as his professed disciple, I stand prepared to do
it. The time for fulfilling this pledge, it seems to me,
has come. Sir, I dare not flee away from Alton.
Should I attempt it, I should feel that the angel of the
Lord, with his flaming sword, was pursuing me where-
ever I went. It is because I fear God, that I am not
afraid of all who oppose me in this city. No, sir, the
contest has commenced here; and here it must be
finished. Before God and you all, I here pledge myself to continue it, if need be, till death. If I fall, my
grave shall be made in Alton."

This dauntless, courageous determination, given forth
calmly, and yet with deep feeling, had a manifest effect
on his audience, and even some of his foes were melted
to tears; but a vigorous effort was made to shake off
the impression, and, so successfully, that before the
close of the meeting, the violent mob-spirit was once
more in the ascendant. The impression he made was
not, however, wholly effaced, and one result of it was,
that the mayor promised to protect the landing and
setting up of the fourth press, which he did at a time
unexpected by the mob. But when the tidings spread
that a new press had arrived, their fury knew no
bounds; the store was attacked, the press seized, and
the building set on fire. Lovejoy was seen, and immediately five balls were lodged in his body, and he
had only time to retire within the building and to die.
His age was thirty-two. At a time when life is dearest,
and most full of promise, in the full vigour of his manhood, he willingly relinquished all to die in the cause

of the oppressed slave, and of the Master who came to " proclaim liberty to the captives, and the opening of the prison to them that are bound." When the noble mother of Lovejoy heard of his death, she said, " It is well; I had rather he would die so, than forsake his principles!" Such were the martyrs, and such the women of the anti-slavery cause in America.

The news of this tragedy awoke feelings of intense indignation even in some of the slave states. In Boston, a requisition, headed by Dr. Channing, and signed by many influential citizens, was drawn up, asking for the use of Faneuil Hall, in which to hold a meeting to express the alarm and horror of the citizens at the outrage on civil liberty, and the murder of a Christian minister for no offence but that of being true to his convictions. The authorities at first refused the petition; a spontaneous meeting was then held to prepare a second requisition, which was so numerously signed that the authorities yielded to it. The meeting was composed of persons of many shades of opinion. It began with prayer, and then discussion followed. A respected citizen, unconnected with any party, Mr. Jonathan Phillips, occupied the chair. It was a momentous time for the abolitionists, as the great mass of people surged with the different opinions of the different speakers. But at length one very young man, of good family, came forth with such masterly and convincing arguments, that the right of free discussion was established for the time; and it was acknowledged that the eloquence of young Wendell Phillips carried the day.

CHAPTER IV.

FREEDOM OF THE PRESS.—WM. SHREVE BAILEY OF KENTUCKY.—OLD
  PIONEER SOCIETY IN 1841.—CHANGE OF TACTICS IN PRO-SLAVERY
  OPPOSITION.—THE TRUE CHURCH.—THE AMERICAN CHURCH.

THE assertion of freedom of the press in the cause
of the slave has often been the ground of bitter persecution to those who maintained it, and suffering has
not ceased on this account, even to this day, in the
United States. We believe very few who have read
even the brief account we have given of Elijah P. Lovejoy, would not have gladly done or given a little to
save him if they could; but he is dead, and all that
can be done for him now is to honour his name by
seeking to imitate his disinterestedness and devotion.
Still our sympathies need not return to lie dormant,
while there are others to claim them; and we wish to
introduce to our readers a living sufferer in very similar circumstances, whom it is still possible to cheer and
assist. We allude to William Shreve Bailey of Newport, Kentucky. He started in that town as a machine
maker, about the year 1849; but this business did not
engross all his thoughts; his sympathies were largely
called forth for the slaves, and he ventured, even in a
Slave State, to plead their cause through the columns
of a newspaper recently started in the town of Newport. These articles excited the wrath of slaveholders
in the neighbourhood, who by threats and violence induced the proprietor of the paper to give up the name
of his obnoxious contributor. Bailey was then visited

in his machine shop and rudely assaulted; and but for the interference of his workmen, his life might have paid the forfeit of his temerity. The proprietor of the paper then alleged that it had been so greatly injured by these transactions that he insisted on Bailey's purchasing the press and printing materials; this was accordingly done, and the *Newport News* was issued from the machine shop in March 1850. The paper succeeded very well for some time, notwithstanding the violent opposition of the neighbouring slaveholders, who, finding all their other efforts to suppress it ineffectual, at last, on the 6th of October 1851, set fire to the premises and burned down the press, machine shop, and all. The loss to Mr. Bailey on this occasion amounted to 16,000 dollars. By the assistance of his workmen he succeeded in setting up another press in his own house and procuring a fresh set of types, and the name of the paper was shortly after changed to the more significant one of the *Free South*. Various expedients were again resorted to to effect his overthrow; his workmen were tampered with to such an extent that they refused to work with him; he then had his own family taught to set types. At first the paper so issued was poor enough, but by degrees his wife and ten children learned to work as well and expeditiously as most of the printers of the town. Thus they laboured on, as a reliable witness writes in 1857 :—" Father, mother, and children, and even the little ones, toiling, amid obloquy, reproach, and savage foes, to redeem their state from the dreadful sin and curse of slavery ! Mortgaging the homestead, working till midnight,

practising the most rigid economy, making their house
a citadel where the weapons of truth must be defended
by the weapons of death; and that not for the sake of
praise, but to honour God, to save slaves and slaveholders, and wipe from Kentucky its foulest blot and
shame. That noble wife and mother, with worn fingers
and wearied limbs, is worthy the man who perils so
much; and those children are greater than the sons of
Sparta or Rome! Such heroism should not go unre-
warded."

In 1859, one of these children, a beloved little girl
of twelve years old, died. The parents thought her
health had suffered by close confinement to the "case;"
but she was so earnest in her work, and her nimble
little fingers set types so well, that they did not
observe her gradual decline. As soon as they noticed
her pale face they sent her to school, to try a change
of occupation. The little one did not even then forget
that she had a mission in life; she told her schoolmates
of the slaves, and how much she pitied them; and then
the parents, who were slaveholders, forbade them to
associate with " the little abolitionist." But her gentle Christian spirit soon drew them round her again,
and she continued to plead for the slave to the last.
However, death had set his seal on her, and very soon
this little girl was taken from a life of privation, toil,
and danger, to hear that inasmuch as she had done it
unto one of the least of his children, she had done it to
her Lord and Redeemer. Her poor father and mother,
brothers and sisters, toiled on, with saddened, wearied
hearts. Again and again were assaults made on the

printing-office, and the press and types injured; prosecution after prosecution was instituted; but the brave hearts would not give up their right to labour for the slave. On the 29th of October, 1859, a last outrage of the kind was perpetrated. The pro-slavery mob—which the night before had forcibly entered the office, carried off the types, and scattered them along the streets,—returned to the assault. Seizing a plank, they battered down the door, entered the house, and took off everything within reach;—amongst other articles, a pocket-book containing nearly all the money poor Bailey had in the world. On this occasion the damage sustained was estimated at 3000 dollars. After describing these scenes he adds very touchingly:—" The heart-rending sorrow of my family, working so many years, night and day, so long as our physical strength would allow, and being harassed by the law for debt (after the destruction of my former office and machine shop by incendiarism), sued for slander because I had published a truth upon a man who had acted unjustly in his official capacity as sheriff—wading through all these trials and troubles of six years' duration, and beginning to be able to live a little more comfortably, we are now fallen upon again, and our whole means of subsistence destroyed. To stand by and behold these ravages, filled the hearts of my family with inexpressible grief. I have transgressed no law of Kentucky, nor do I intend to do so; but I ask protection from lawless violence in the legitimate publication of my paper. I dislike the taking up of arms, even in self-defence; but for the righteousness of my

E

cause, the dignity of my state, and the honour of my people, I shall maintain my position and labour, and I ask the friends of true American liberty to aid me. The spirit of freedom and true greatness is beginning to be planted upon Kentucky soil, and it ill becomes the legal authorities to stand aloof and suffer the freedom of speech and of the press to be trampled under foot, to stifle that liberty which tyrants in all ages have sought to overthrow."

Even after this assault, the press was again repaired, the types gathered up from the streets; and, with a little delay, once more the *Free South* was issued. But scarcely had it appeared, when, in the most unexpected manner, its fearless editor was seized, and committed to prison on the charge of issuing incendiary publications—an unfounded charge, as a perusal of the offending number of the *Free South*, now lying before us, would abundantly prove. Bail was obtained for him, and Bailey was liberated for the time. Some of his New England friends sent him across the Atlantic, in order that he might interest the British friends of the slave in his case. His permitted period of absence was so short that all his visit could accomplish was to awaken a little sympathy for himself and family. He returned in time to relieve his bail and stand his trial. The trial was, however, again postponed, and its issue may be less severe to him than was anticipated, from the altered position of affairs in that part of the United States. But in the meantime he is suffering terribly from the pecuniary pressure his losses have entailed on him, and he fears he will scarcely be able to hold his ground. Another appeal has been made for him to his friends, and surely it ought not to be made in vain. The last tidings received from William S. Bailey mention 'the death of a son, twenty-one years of age, who fell a victim to cold and exposure while serving in the Union army; he was a faithful abolitionist, and while in the hospital indoctrinated his companions into the promise that " they would ever be good to the poor slaves if they had a chance." The letter also mentions the death of Margaret, a daughter of eighteen. She was the sweet singer of the family, and her favourite melodies were those that told of the slaves' sufferings. She died of brain fever, brought on by excitement, anxiety, and hardship, and her death was a severe blow to the poor mother, and, adds the father, " These losses and toils were hard for us to bear up under; but I am glad I am still here in Kentucky to hold my ground."

To return now in some degree to the chronological order of our narrative. In 1841 the report of the Massachusetts Anti-Slavery Society opens by " reverently acknowledging the superintending care of the Almighty over the interests of the enterprise which it is their privilege to espouse, and which they cannot doubt must eventually obtain a splendid triumph over all opposition." It tells us that two thousand kindred societies had sprung from it, and concludes by urging " the friends of bleeding humanity to go onward in the strength of God, turning neither to the right hand nor to the left, *clinging to duty more closely than to life,* and extending their operations for the downfall of

slavery. Their object is definite, grand, glorious; their
principles are true and unconquerable; and they have
only to persevere a little longer, in faith and hope,
and the voices of emancipated millions of their country-
men will be heard thundering heavenward—Slavery is
ended, is ended! and we are free! alleluiah! for the
Lord God Omnipotent reigneth!"

Such was the spirit of the abolitionists. It was well
for them that they did not foresee that at least twenty-
one years of hard toil, persecution, and obloquy, were
yet before them; strengthened by their firm faith in
the goodness of their cause, and in Him who was
emphatically its leader, they went on steadfastly. The
success of their efforts had been wonderful, their periodicals had been scattered by millions over the land,
and the anti-slavery idea had been propagated most
industriously and successfully. Yet pro-slavery animosity was not *abated*, but *increased*, by the success
of the anti-slavery enterprise. The time had gone by
when the Northern States could tolerate the personal
violence, the peril of life and limb to which abolitionists had been subjected, and although the price of 5000
dollars was set on the head of W. L. Garrison, and a
still larger sum on that of Arthur Tappan, no attempt
was ever made to claim these rewards—the pro-slavery
emissaries in the North did not venture so far. The
persecutions now adopted were of a more subtle character—not so intelligible, and not so easily met.

We have before alluded to the subserviency of the
great religious denominations, both North and South,
to slavery. In the outset of the struggle, W. L. Garri-

son thought he would have nothing to do but to present the case of the slave to the professed ministers of him " *who came to preach deliverance to the captives.*" He fully acknowledged the power of the clergy, and went from door to door begging them to espouse the cause of the oppressed; but he found everywhere a deaf ear turned to the cry of the slave, and he went sorrowfully away, his hopes crushed in that direction, and a conviction awakened in his mind that the *American* Church was not the Church of Christ. The natural contemplation of the *true Church,* under these circumstances, refreshed and cheered him. He has given his thoughts on this subject in the following sonnet :—

" THE TRUE CHURCH.

" Church of the living God ! in vain thy foes
  Make thee in impious mirth their laughing-stock,
  Contemn thy strength, thy radiant beauty mock;
In vain their threats, and impotent their blows—
Satan's assaults—Hell's agonizing throes !
  For thou art built upon the Eternal Rock,
  Nor fear'st the thunder-storm—the earthquake shock;
And nothing shall disturb thy calm repose.
All human combinations change and die,
  Whate'er their origin, name, form, design;
But firmer than the pillars of the sky,
  Thou standest ever by a Power divine :
Thou art endowed with Immortality,
  And canst not perish—GOD'S OWN LIFE IS THINE !"

Albert Barnes, the great commentator, has affirmed " that there was no power *out* of the church which could sustain slavery an hour, if it was not sustained *in* it;" and so, as the church would not put forth the power which it possessed, to *suppress* slavery, but, on the other hand, gave all its influence to *sustain* it, the abolitionists felt called upon to rebuke its course, and many of them eventually withdrew from its fellowship. This was the signal for a great amount of persecution, which was extended towards all who, whether within the ranks of the abolitionists or outside of them, felt called to plead for the slave, and in so doing to administer an implied, if not an actual, censure on the false church of the United States. The loss of reputation, with ecclesiastical and social reproach, were in many cases harder to bear than personal assaults and imprisonments, and it was well for the abolitionists that they had learned to say with the psalmist, "In God have I put my trust—I will not be afraid what man can do unto me." Thus they fearlessly pursued their mission of proclaiming the chosen fast of the Lord, "To undo the heavy burdens, and to let the oppressed go free, and that ye break every yoke." This mission should have been that of the church, but she had refused!

It is scarcely necessary for us to give very many proofs of the pro-slavery character of the American Church and the great religious organizations; suffice it to say, that in the South ministers and members of orthodox churches held slaves to the number of at least 660,000. The cruelties perpetrated on these poor sufferers were not the less ferocious because of their reputed owners professing to be *Christians!* Slaves have been sold, and for aught we know are still sold, for the support of missions to the *heathen;* theological seminaries have been endowed by legacies in slaves;

and worst of all, " men quote Scripture for the deed,"
and, as Mrs. Stowe says, " baptize slavery in the name
of the Father, Son, and Holy Ghost." We refer our
readers to the easily-accessible " Key to Uncle Tom's
Cabin " for abundance of well-authenticated facts to
prove that, although " the trader does the repulsive
work, the Southern Church defends him—the Northern
Church defends the South—every one does as much
for slavery as would be at all expedient, considering
the latitude they live in. This is the practical result
of the thing." The strong objection of the clergy of
the South to having the anti-slavery question agitated
may be illustrated by one or two quotations. The
Rev. Thomas S. Witherspoon, a member of the Presbyterian Church, says,—" I draw my warrant from the
Scriptures of the Old and New Testament, to hold the
slave in bondage. The principle of holding the heathen
in bondage is recognised by God. When the tardy
process of the law is too long in redressing our griev-
ances, we of the South have adopted the summary
remedy of Judge Lynch; and really, I think it is one
of the most wholesome and salutary remedies for the
malady of Northern fanaticism that can be devised. I
go to the Bible for my warrant in all moral matters.
Let your emissaries dare to venture across the Potomac, and I cannot promise you that their fate will be
less than Haman's." The Rev. Robert N. Anderson,
also a member of the Presbyterian Church, says, in a
letter to the Sessions of the Presbyterian congregations
within the bounds of the West Hanover Presbytery,—
" Now, dear Christian brethren, I humbly express it

as my earnest wish that you quit yourselves like men.
If there be any stray goat of a minister among you
tainted with the bloodhound principles of abolitionism,
let him be ferreted out, silenced, excommunicated, and
left to the public to dispose of him in other respects.
—Your affectionate brother in the Lord, Robert N.
Anderson."

Such were the characteristic declarations of Churches
of the South, and the Northern Church fellowshipped
them, and in somewhat modified terms took similar
grounds. The Philadelphia Annual Methodist Con-
ference, under date 7th April 1847, to the societies
under its care, in a sort of apologetic letter, says :
" Some suspect us of being abolitionists. We would
ask your brethren, Whether the question we have
been accustomed for a few years past to put to candi-
dates for admission amongst us, namely, Are you an
Abolitionist? and without each one answering in the
negative, he was not received, ought not to protect us
from this charge ? Whether the action of the last con-
ference on this matter ought not to satisfy any fair and
candid.mind that we are not, and do not desire to be,
abolitionists ?

" J. P. DARBIN.   WM. H. GILDER.

J. KENNEDY.   JOSEPH CASTLE."

IGNATIUS T. COOPER.

The Presbyterian and other Churches of the North
adopted similar action, both negatively and positively.
The power of the Church was used to suppress those
struggling minorities, who, within its own borders,

sought to purify it of its sins. The anti-slavery resolutions and overtures that were offered at the annual conclaves were scornfully repressed or vehemently rejected, not unfrequently, indeed, resulting in more stringent rules against the discussion of the question; and there are many instances of ministers being deposed from their pulpit for no other offence than that of remembering the slave as bound with him, and of opening their mouths for the dumb. One of the victims of this ecclesiastical tyranny was the late lamented Dudley Tyng of Philadelphia, son of Dr. Tyng of New York; and so recently as the autumn of 1861, the Rev. Mr. Fowler, pastor of a Presbyterian Church at Auburn, New York, who had been convinced that it was his duty to remember the slaves in his prayers, was visited with severe censure, and finally expelled from the Church.

In some cases this ecclesiastical persecution assumed a different form. When the minister was of too high a standing to be dismissed summarily, another plan was tried; the congregations were acted on by pro-slavery influences to demand the resignation of the minister, and if this was not successful, persecutions in many forms ensued. Of such a character were those which assailed Dr. Cheever. Sound in theology, earnest and eloquent as a Christian minister, he was greatly beloved by his large congregation, till, like his Master, he felt the Spirit of the Lord upon him, compelling him to preach deliverance to the captive. Then ensued persecution after persecution to induce him to abandon his pulpit, but he stood firm, feeling that

there he had a vantage-ground from which to plead
the cause of the oppressed; then his wealthy supporters
one after another deserted him, and pecuniary pressure
was tried; but he has been able, by the blessing of
God on his efforts, and the sympathy of friends beyond
the Church, to continue to this day.   Others have not
been so successful; and the Omniscient alone can number the gentle, earnest, faithful Abdiels who have stood
for His cause in the midst of a reprobate Church, whose
hearts have drooped from the heat of persecution, and
whose comfort has been derived only from the presence
of Him who in all their afflictions was afflicted; their
efforts and words have not been in vain, and the great
day of account may reveal them in their true value.

The great religious organizations of the United
States bowed down to the same pro-slavery influences;
the American Board of Commissioners of Foreign Missions, the American Bible Society, the Sunday-school
Union, and the American Tract Society, all ignored
the slaves and fraternized with their oppressors.   The
Bible Society refused to supply Bibles to the slaves,
but accepted the brotherly aid of their taskmasters,
who decreed death for the second offence of teaching
them to read its messages of comfort and salvation.
The Tract Society, by expunging from standard works
all references to slavery, suited their publications to
their slaveholding patrons.   One of the most remarkable instances of this sort of expurgation occurs in the
recent publication, at Philadelphia, of an edition of the
Book of Common Prayer.   Marked by the authentic
imprimatur of the Right Rev. George W. Doane, Bishop

of New Jersey, this edition introduces as a frontispiece Ary Scheffer's beautiful picture of " *Christus Conso-lator.*" This well-known picture represents the Saviour seated with the emblems of his Divine compassion around Him,—the wretched beings whose sorrows he had ministered to, whose diseases he had cured. There is the mother laying her dead infant at the sacred feet; the sick man imploring the healing of the Al-mighty touch; the maniac just restored to reason with the broken chain in his Deliverer's grasp; the young widow leaning upon him; the negro slave holding out his fettered hands for deliverance. In this new Phila-delphia edition, to suit Southern readers, THE FIGURE OF THE NEGRO IS LEFT OUT. Thus Church and State in America have united in their endeavours to blot out this child of God, not only from his place among the nations of the earth, but also from his place of privilege as a humble suppliant for the mercy and consolation of the blessed Saviour, whose mission of love so emphatically included him,—the bruised, the bound, the broken-hearted.

CHAPTER V.

FUGITIVE SLAVES AND THEIR HELPERS.—JOHN L. BROWN CONDEMNED
TO DEATH FOR AIDING THE ESCAPE OF A COLOURED GIRL.—REV.
CHARLES TURNER TORREY. — UNDERGROUND RAILROAD. — THE
BRANDED HAND.—FRANCIS JACKSON, ESQ., OF BOSTON.—REV. CAL-
VIN FAIRBANKS.—MEXICAN WAR.—ANNEXATION OF TEXAS.—
MISSOURI COMPROMISE.—CONSTITUTIONAL SUPPORT OF SLAVERY.—
MORAL REVOLUTION PRINCIPLES.

DURING the whole anti-slavery struggle, perhaps the
most violent persecutions have been endured by those
who have aided in the escape of slaves. Even before
the passing of the Fugitive Slave Law, the free states
were bound, by one of the clauses of the United States'
constitution, to return slaves that had escaped to their
master; the law of God was set aside, and the poor
victims of oppression were returned to more hopeless
and cruel bondage than before. Even in the free
states, those who took the part of the slave had to
suffer imprisonment, fines, and the spoiling of their
goods. In the Southern States these persecutions
have been fearful. In 1844, John L. Brown was condemned to death by the governor of South Carolina,
for attempting to aid the escape of a young coloured
woman, to whom he was greatly attached. They were
seen walking together, and poor Brown was tried and
sentenced to death. Some of our readers may recollect
the indignation which was aroused in Great Britain
on intelligence of this atrocious sentence. Public
meetings were held, the first of which took place, we
believe, in Edinburgh; the example spread, and Lord

Brougham brought forward the matter in the House of Lords. British public opinion prevailed even with the governor of South Carolina; the sentence was first commuted from the penalty of death to that of receiving fifty lashes; and even this punishment was afterwards remitted, on condition of Brown's leaving the state. This illustration of the influence of British public sentiment is very striking, and must excite a feeling of regret that this power has so often been suffered to remain idle, or on some melancholy occasions (such as fellowshipping pro-slavery Churches), to lean to the other side. We trust that now when liberty is struggling convulsively for the mastery, Britain will unmistakably stand by the slave; this position of hers will influence the North and overawe the South much more efficaciously than interposition on either side could do.

The Rev. Charles Turner Torrey is the next sufferer whom we shall introduce to our readers. He was born on the 1st November 1813. After being educated to the ministry, he found that his vocation comprehended an uncompromising devotion to the cause of the slave and a hatred of oppression. In America, persecution necessarily followed the fearless carrying out of his convictions, and in 1842 he was imprisoned at Annapolis in Maryland, for showing himself on the side of the coloured people. It was during this incarceration that he had a quiet time to reduce to a system the time-honoured institution of the " Underground Rail road." The escape of slaves had been aided wisely and faithfully from the earliest days; but the *name* was

given after a regular plan had been arranged of hand-
ing on the poor fugitive from one benevolent and
trustworthy agent at *stations on the line* to another,
so the chain was completed from the slave states to
Canada. After Mr. Torrey's liberation, he proceeded
to carry out in detail the outline he had formed, and
so successful was he, that before many weeks were
over, the line was completed from the slave states to
Canada, a distance varying from two hundred to five
hundred miles, with all its machinery of vigilance
committees, spies, pilots, conveyances, and signals.
The arrangements were so perfect, that the slaveholders were utterly confounded in their pursuit of the
slaves, and could find no solution of the mystery except in the supposition that their *property* must have
been spirited away by a *subterranean road.* They
thus gave the name to a scheme which has proved itself
one of the most honourable institutions of the United
States of America.

The Traffic of the Underground Railroad has been
very continuous. Before the passage of the Fugitive
Slave Law, the average number of passengers exceeded
a thousand a year; after that time it greatly increased,
partly because the slaves, by some remarkable medium
of intelligence, became aware that if they struck a certain line they would be helped to Canada, and partly
because the odious law called forth sympathy for the
fugitives, and many friends and helpers throughout
the free states. Mr. Torrey continued to work this
institution, and he rejoiced that by his direct instru-
mentality four hundred human beings had gained their

liberty, the greater part of whom, but for his exertions, would probably have died in slavery. For his labours for them, however, he himself suffered and died. On the 25th of June 1844 he was arrested at Baltimore on a charge of helping sundry slaves to escape. After long delay and a three days' trial, on the testimony of perjured witnesses he was sentenced to six years' imprisonment in the penitentiary. In the autumn of 1845 his health began to fail, and on the 9th of May 1846 he died a martyr to the cause of the slave.

About the same period, and for the same offence, that of aiding the escape of slaves, three other individuals, Messrs. Thompson, Work, and Burr, were sentenced to be imprisoned for three years. Their families were left in deep distress, and they themselves suffered greatly in health.

In 1844, Captain Jonathan Walker allowed seven slaves to sail with him in his vessel from Pensacola, in West Florida. Owing to illness he was unable to navigate his boat, which was captured and sent back to Pensacola. The slaves were returned to their owners and Captain Walker was put in prison, when he nearly lost his life through the severity of his treatment during his illness. He was afterwards tried, convicted, and placed in the pillory, where the letters S. S. (slave stealer) were branded on his hand with a red-hot iron. Captain Walker afterwards published a narrative entitled "The Branded Hand," which elicited much sympathy, and led others to follow in his course.

It was in 1844 that Francis Jackson, a Boston merchant (he who, in 1833, had opened his house to

receive the Ladies' Anti-Slavery Society, when almost
all others were closed against them), resigned his com-
mission of the peace on the following ground:—He
maintained that the call of duty and humanity was in
favour of the slave and not of the master; and in his
letter of resignation to Governor Briggs, he makes this
declaration: "That part of the constitution which pro-
vides for the surrender of fugitive slaves I never have
supported, and never will. I will join in no slave-
hunt. My door shall stand open, as it has long stood,
for the panting and trembling victim of the slave-
hunter. When I shut my door against him, may God
shut the door of his mercy against me."

In the same year the Rev. Calvin Fairbanks was
arrested for aiding slaves to escape, and was sentenced
to fifteen years' imprisonment. He was, however,
liberated in 1849. After that time he resided in Massachusetts and New York, till about the year 1851,
when he was impelled to visit the grave of his father,
who died at Lexington in 1849, when he went to present a petition on behalf of his son to the legislature of
Kentucky. Fairbanks was suddenly seized, without
any legal proof, on an alleged charge of aiding slaves,
and was sentenced to fifteen years' imprisonment;
and his sufferings were very great, owing to the hostility of the authorities.

The annexation of Texas in 1846, followed by the
Mexican war in 1847, added greatly to the strength
of the slave power, for both were planned for the interests of slavery. The abolitionists had exerted every
effort to preserve their country from these calamities,

but in vain. These extensions of slave territory not only afforded fresh soil on which to plant slavery, but politically increased the power of slaveholders. Attempts were made in congress to insert a clause in the bill for admitting Texas to the union, to the effect of prohibiting slavery there for ever; but this was vetoed, and Texas was allowed to enter the union as soon as it should have formed a constitution, with or without slavery. The only concession made to abolitionists was, that in any states that might hereafter be formed out of the territory north of the *Missouri line of compromise*, slavery or involuntary servitude should be for ever prohibited.

Perhaps it may be interesting to refer briefly to this compromise line, which in after days had so much to do with the cause of freedom. The Missouri compromise was effected in the year 1820, when that state applied to be admitted into the union. The question of restriction was mooted, and it was proposed that Missouri should only be allowed to enter the union with a constitutional clause prohibiting slavery in the state. Warm debates ensued, and it was argued that it was inexpedient and unjust that the new state should be trammelled by any restrictions to prevent its free entrance into the union as soon as the constitution should be formed. This plea ultimately succeeded, and Missouri became a slave state; but as a conciliatory measure to the restriction party, it was determined by vote of Congress that slavery *should not be extended to the territories of the United States north and west of Missouri*, the line of limit to slavery being 36° 30'.

F

In 1836, Missouri, in violation of treaties with the
Indians, succeeded in annexing a very fertile addition
to the *west* of the prescribed line. A bill empowering
this annexation was smuggled through Congress, and
this rich acquisition, sufficient to form seven counties,
became slave territory, and the most productive portion of the State of Missouri. It was from this corner
that, twenty years afterwards, the "ruffians" crossed
into Kansas to perpetrate those outrages yet recent in
our memories. And it was with the usual violations of
good faith where slavery was concerned, that an attempt was made to *repeal* this compromise, so as to
admit of the extension of slavery to Kansas and Nebraska. That attempt called forth the indignant resistance of Kansas, which was at length successful,
after years of struggle, when that state was admitted
to the union *free*. These circumstances form a remarkable link in the anti-slavery chain of events which
have culminated in the present state of matters in the
United States. But we have anticipated, in order to
show the connexion of the Missouri compromise with
the anti-slavery struggles of after days.

We must now return to the abolitionists. They
very soon began to discover that there was no hope
for the slave from the legislature and its enactments;
every measure which in the most remote degree tended
to the abolition of slavery was thrown out, and the
slaveholders ruled the government of the United States.
The so-called *free* states submitted tamely to the pro-
slavery domination, and sustained the South in its
slaveholding position. This course naturally led the

abolitionists to analyze the constitution of the United States, which acted as a compact to bind North and South in common cause to oppress a whole race of human beings on their soil.

The Declaration of Independence had proclaimed that " all men are born free and equal, and are endowed by the Creator with certain inalienable rights, among which are life, liberty, and the pursuit of happiness." A noble preamble truly for the basis of government of a new nation! Surely it indicated a guarantee that a death-blow to slavery was struck. But when the provisions of the constitution were framed, eleven years after the declaration of independence, it was seen that this declaration meant no more than that all *white* men are born free and equal, and that only *white* men are endowed by the Creator with certain inalienable rights. Black men, on the other hand, were then understood, and were afterwards expressly declared, " to *have no rights* which white men are bound to respect." Although the word *slave* is not found throughout the clauses of the constitution, yet distinct provisions are found there for the protection of slave property, which have been acted on by the whole of the United States ever since they were formed into a nation.

As John Quincy Adams, ex-president of the United States, says, " it cannot be denied that the slaveholding lords of the South prescribed, as a condition of their assent to the constitution, three special provisions to secure the perpetuity of their dominion over their slaves: — 1. The immunity for twenty years of the

F F

African slave-trade; 2. The stipulation to surrender
fugitive slaves, an engagement positively prohibited
by the laws of God from Sinai; and 3. The exaction
of a representation for slaves—for articles of merchandise under the name of *persons*." Besides the articles
which provide for these requirements of the slaveholder,
another was added, binding the president to employ
the naval, military, ordnance, and militia resources of
the entire country for the suppression of slave insur-
rections. The slave representation clause may require
a brief explanation. It provided (Art. I. sect. 2) for
the representation of all free white persons, and for
that of *three-fifths of all other persons* (these persons
meant the *slaves*), and this clause acted as a political
premium on slaveholding, for free men in a slave state,
solely because they were slaveholders, had a larger representation, and consequently greater political power
than the same number of persons in a free state. Thus
one man, the owner of ten slaves, counted as much in
the basis of representation as seven men who held no
slaves; and the 300,000 slaveholders of the United
States virtually represented as many votes as 2,100,000
free men who held no slaves. In reference to these
constitutional guarantees to slavery, well might John
Quincy Adams assert, that " the preservation, propa-
gation, and perpetuity of slavery is the vital and animating principle of the national government, and that
a knot of slaveholders give the law and prescribe the
policy of the country."

Such being the state of the case, the advanced party
of abolitionists found no hope for the slave in the Con-

stitution as they understood it, and as it had been interpreted and acted on for seventy-two years. Gradually their convictions on this point took another direction, which greatly affected their position in society. With the views they held of the pro-slavery character of the American constitution, they could not conscientiously support it themselves, and as a natural sequence could not conscientiously appoint other men to a position in which the first step would be to swear to maintain this constitution and to carry out its provisions: to return fugitives to bondage, to order out the United States' army and navy to suppress slave insurrection, &c., and in other respects aid in the extension and perpetuation of slavery. They therefore declined voting, renouncing, for the sake of the slave and their own conscience, that political right so dear to Americans. This renunciation was not without its reward in an increased clearness of moral vision and an increased amount of moral power. Standing apart from the excitement of politics, they could see more distinctly the bearings of the various political measures and agencies that affected the cause of the slave; they faithfully discussed those measures, and earnestly considered the obstacles that interposed in the way of emancipation. The most mighty of these was a blind idolatry of the Union, which led Northern men to make degrading concessions and compromises to the South; in fact, in order to preserve the union the North were willing to preserve slavery also, and to bow down to it and serve it. Then it became evident to the watchers that the union must be severed before

slavery could be abolished. Their idea was that the
North should by common consent withdraw from this
unholy alliance, " insisting on the abolition of slavery
or the dissolution of the union," and to this end their
very earnest efforts were directed. Their prophetic
vision was right, that the dissolution of the union must
precede the abolition of slavery; but as yet they could
not foresee the method of this dissolution. They did
not anticipate that it was the South that should secede
from the North, and that this secession should be confirmed by war and death and desolation.

The number of abolitionists who adopted the non-
voting principle was very small, but they had great
moral power. In the year 1845, when this principle of
no union with slaveholders was adopted, their report
says, " A revolution is begun which never will, which
never can go backwards. Our work is not yet done.
It is but begun. Our business is still the same as at
the beginning, to sound for ever the tale of the wrongs
of the slave and their own guilt in the ears of the people, whether they will hear or whether they will for-
bear. We may never be numerous, but we shall always
be enough to make the general conscience uneasy until
it has purified the nation of its guilt. Our conflict is
one in which success is not in proportion to the numbers, but to the faithfulness of those who engage in it.
We can look for no reward or glory as the world calls
such; next to the satisfaction of doing our duty to
God and man as we find it lying before us at our
doors, it is a just and animating excitement to feel
that we are permitted to partake in a passage of the

world's history which can never be forgotten, which will affect the condition of millions till time is no more, and which will extend its influences into the unknown expanse of eternity."

The admission of Texas as a slave state to the union in 1846, following on the previous admissions of Louisiana and Florida, and the Mexican war undertaken in 1847 to strengthen the slave power, confirmed the abolitionists in their opinion that " slavery ruled the destinies of the American people because they loved to have it so." They then add : " It is our business to give them no peace in their wickedness, to set their sins for ever in order before them, to demonstrate to them the folly of their crimes. *When the necessary revolution in the mind of the people is completed, that in the institutions of the country will follow, as the day the night.* Although we cannot foresee the exact time, nor the precise way in which American slavery will be abolished, we know that its doom is sealed, for we believe that God is just. It is only a question of time and of instruments. The abolition of slavery we recognise as the great task assigned to this generation in this country. We accept it as our appointed work, and are grateful to be permitted to assist in the evolution of this magnificent event. Never was a nobler task assigned to man. The scorn of the world, the anathema of the Church, the sacrifice of the vulgar objects of ambition, may be well endured for the promotion of a cause, in the issues of which are involved the deliverance of the slave, the redemption of the country, and the progress of the race."

CHAPTER VI.

IN 1848 occurred some very remarkable and interesting cases of suffering in the cause of freedom, of which
we must give a short outline.   On the 13th of March
of that year news reached Washington that the revolution in France had resulted in the establishment of a
republic instead of a monarchy, and the citizens, in the
enthusiasm of sympathy, held meetings and passed
resolutions in which this *triumph of liberty* was celebrated, while torch-light processions and illuminations
further signalized the event.   Hearing freedom so
highly exalted, it was not wonderful that a practical
application of the theory was attempted by some who
as yet had known nothing of it but the name.   Seventy-
seven slaves, in quest of the boon so loudly praised,
sought the assistance of a fearless man, who thought
it better to *do* something for freedom than to make
speeches about it, and he favoured their escape.   This
man was Capt. Drayton, who commanded the schooner
Pearl, which cast anchor on the memorable 13th in the
Potomac at Washington.   His mate, Mr. Sayers, was
like-minded with himself, and under their protection
these seventy-seven men and women in fear and trem-

bling, yet with hope in their hearts, embarked on board
the little schooner, which pursued its way in safety for
two hundred miles, and they thought that liberty was
gained. But, alas! the shouters for freedom at Washington had discovered that these prisoners had escaped,
and with *worthy consistency* had despatched a steamer
armed with two hundred fighting men to bring back
the fugitives to bondage; and when they reached Washington the excitement of satisfaction in this re-capture,
this triumph of practical despotism, was equal to that
in behalf of French revolutionary liberty which had
prevailed three days before. The poor victims were
remanded for sale to the far South, and the men who
had aided them were only saved from the murderous
vengeance of the infuriated populace by being lodged
in jail to await their trial for the deed they had committed. There they were subjected to the harshest
and most unjustifiable treatment till the end of July,
when they were brought up for trial, and a sentence
was awarded which was equivalent to life-long imprisonment, and this because they had followed the dictates of kind hearts and Christian charity. Unwearied
exertions were made in their behalf, without the slightest apparent result. Year after year passed on, they
still pined in prison, and their friends were almost in
despair, when most unexpectedly their petitions were
answered, and the prisoners were discharged in 1852,
pardoned by Millard Filmore, in consequence of the
able and earnest efforts of the Hon. Charles Sumner.

It is not quite within the province of these outlines
to dwell on the particular cases of the seventy-seven

who sought freedom on board the *Pearl,* but many of them were of the most touching description. Foremost among them was that of the six children of the Edmondson family, which has been graphically given by Mrs. Stowe in the Key to Uncle Tom's Cabin; but its incidents are so interesting, that we may be allowed slightly to revive them, if only to illustrate the nature of the offence for which Drayton and Sayers suffered such heavy penalties.

The father and mother, Paul and Milly Edmondson, resided in the neighbourhood of Washington. Paul had received his freedom; and although Milly was still a slave, she was allowed to live with him in their own little house till their children were grown up and had become intelligent refined Christian men and women. It was a life-long agony to Milly to bring up those children, knowing that they were not hers, and dreading the face of every white man who approached their dwelling, lest he came to buy them. Paul comforted her, and encouraged her to do all she could to train them as God's children, and if they were heirs of the kingdom, it would not so much signify if they were rent away from them on earth; and so the greatest care was taken to teach them the law of the Lord, and to make them love freedom. As they grew up they were hired out in the neighbourhood, and were still under their parents' eyes. They were said to be the finest family for miles round, and *their value in the market was fifteen thousand dollars!* Think of it, Christian fathers and mothers, who toil late and early with faith and prayer that *your* children may be " heirs of the kingdom," how could you bear to have them priced in the market, bodies and souls, at fifteen thousand dollars (£3000) the lot! The mother's teachings of love of freedom so influenced her children, that the two eldest daughters raised money to purchase their own freedom before they married, lest they too should be mothers of slave children. These teachings also influenced six of the others (Mary and Emily, aged respectively fourteen and sixteen years, and their four elder brothers) when, to escape the danger of being sold away, they embarked in search of liberty on board the schooner *Pearl*. The agony to these refined young men and women, when they were re-captured, can scarcely be imagined, but it was terrible. They were hurried through Washington to the slave pens at Alexandria, there to wait four weeks in fearful suspense for Southern purchasers. The brief interviews with friends were heart-rending. They were afterwards taken to Baltimore, then to New Orleans; and no proper purchaser offering, they were again returned to Alexandria. During all this period they had to endure many hardships; and what most distressed the graceful young girls, was the rude character of the examinations to which they were subjected when any intending purchaser came to treat for them. The brothers made representations about it to the dealers, which had the effect of afterwards preventing this brutal treatment.

During their sufferings together, the touching consideration of these brothers and sisters for each other indicated their refinement and family affection. They contrived, by getting up before it was day, to hold a little prayer-meeting together, and thus their hearts were strengthened, and a prayer-hearing God in due time answered their petitions, and those of their devoted parents, for their freedom on earth. Paul Edmondson went to the North, and by earnest representations of the case to anti-slavery friends, and by enlisting on behalf of his children the eloquence of the Rev. Henry Ward Beecher, sufficient money was raised to purchase the freedom of the two girls; and eventually, after a long period of patient effort, anxiety, and prayer, that of the whole family was secured. Thus six of the passengers of the *Pearl*, after months of intense distress, were saved and freed; but sadly different was the fate of most of the other poor sufferers. Very few were purchased, and the rest were sent into hopeless bondage, families separated in an agony of grief, and untold miseries surrounding their life-long slavery.

We may be allowed to mention just one other case; it is that of Emily Russell, another of the passengers of the *Pearl* on that fatal 13th of March. Emily was the daughter of a pious woman who by her industry had succeeded in raising money to purchase her own freedom and that of some of her children. She had gone to New York, where she worked very hard, hoping some day to redeem the rest. Emily was at Washington, a slave, a beautiful young quadroon, with gentle disposition and a heart touched with holy influences. She was on the point of becoming a member of a Christian Church, but she longed for her mother and freedom and safety from the horrors of slavery; so she too embarked in the schooner *Pearl*, and she too was brought

back and destined to be sold at the high price such
qualifications as hers would bring. Her letter to her
mother from Alexandria was most agonising. The
poor mother showed it to friends in New York, who
wrote to Messrs. Bruin & Hill to inquire the price they
would take to release this gentle, refined, Christian
girl. They could not afford to sell her, théy said, under
eighteen hundred dollars, because " she was the most
beautiful woman in the country." This enormous sum
appalled the friends in New York, and before any
thing could be done the coffle had started south, and
poor Emily, sick and heart-broken, in loneliness and
sorrow, on the dreadful journey, yielded up her soul to
God and died, happy in her release from bondage and
her entrance into the presence of the Lamb of God.
The slave-dealers wrote to New York that the girl
Emily was dead. To William Harned of that city was
entrusted the task of telling the news to the stricken
mother. When, in reply to her eager inquiries, he
answered plainly, " Emily is dead," she clasped her
hands in thanksgiving, saying, " The Lord be thanked,
he has heard my prayers at last !" These are but sam-
ples of the cases of the seventy-five who sought refuge
in flight on that memorable day; and it was to save
such as these from the horrors of slavery that the brave
Drayton and Sayers risked their own lives, property,
and freedom; and it was for this act of humanity that
they were sentenced in the *free republican* United
States to expiate their offence by a life-long imprisonment. What wonder that a day of retribution has
come !

These transactions taking place in the district of Columbia (the twelve miles square in which the national capital is situated), very naturally excited the shame of the better thinking members of congress, and prompted efforts to prevent their repetition. Mr. Palfrey, Mr. Giddings, and Mr. Gott of New York, moved respectively for the abolition of slavery in the District—for a bill to authorise its people, blacks and whites, to express their sentiments on the point—and for a bill *to abolish the Slave-trade in the District.* The first two motions were lost of course; the last was carried by a majority of eleven, amid great excitement; but the preamble of the measure was remitted to a " committee of the whole " and was never realised; yet these efforts were not without their value.

It was in the same year, 1848, that Thomas Garrett and John Hunn of Delaware, both members of the Society of Friends, were tried and convicted of the crime of sheltering and conveying from one place to another a poor black woman and her six children, whom the chief-justice had discharged, proof not being had that they were slaves. For this offence Thomas Garrett was fined 5400 dollars and J. Hunn 2500 dollars. Thomas Garrett's defence on the trial, in his simple Quaker language, is worthy to be put beside the highest eloquence. After stating the case briefly and clearly, and showing that it was not *proved* that the fugitives were *slaves,* he added, " But if I had *known every one of them to be slaves, I should have done the same thing.* I should have done violence to my convictions of duty if I had not made use of all the

lawful means in my power to liberate those people, and
to assist them to become men and women, rather than
leave them in the condition of chattels personal. I am
called an abolitionist, once a name of reproach, but one
I am ever proud to be considered worthy of being
called. For the last twenty-five years I have been
much engaged in the cause of this much injured race,
but owing to a multiplicity of other engagements, I
could not devote so much time and mind to their cause
as I otherwise should have done. I am now placed in
a situation in which I have not so much to claim my
attention as formerly (alluding to the loss of his worldly
wealth, by having to sell his farm to meet the legal
penalty and costs imposed on him), and I now pledge
myself, in the presence of this assembly, to use all lawful and honourable means to lessen the burdens of this
oppressed people, and endeavour, according to ability
furnished, to burst their chains asunder and set them
free." The marshal tauntingly said he hoped Mr. Garrett would now mind his own business and not meddle
with slaves again. The reply was characteristic : after
stating that he had assisted over 1400 in twenty-five
years on their way to the North, he added, " I now
consider the penalty imposed may be regarded as a
licence for the rest of my life; but be that as it may, if
any of you know of any poor slave who needs assistance, send him to me; as I now publicly pledge myself
to double my diligence, and never neglect an opportunity to assist a slave to freedom." And well did this
Christian hero redeem his pledge; by day and by night
his labours and vigilance were unfailing; we often find

him watching all night by the bridge from hour to hour, to warn and protect the panting fugitives when danger was at hand; and when immediate alarm was removed, to shelter, to cheer, to clothe, to feed, and send them on their way to freedom.

After a time of difficulty and poverty, he started again in business in 1850, with a borrowed cash capital of less than 1000 dollars; but he had capital of another sort, an unfailing bank of faith and trust, and the blessing of Him who loveth the righteous; and in 1854 he writes, " I have paid my interest, supported my family, and saved 7000 dollars in three years and a half, so I am not so badly off as has been supposed." At that date he mentioned he had passed on to freedom one thousand eight hundred and fifty-three slaves through his station of the Underground Railway, and adds, " Thou wilt perceive I am not either worn out or disheartened in the service." On 17th January, 1860, the legislature of Maryland had it before them to offer a reward for the apprehension of the " arch-traitor" Thomas Garrett, but he has as yet escaped imprisonment; he has aided nearly three thousand slaves to gain their freedom, and still lives, though an old man, to enjoy the blessing of those who were ready to perish.

Great as have been the penalties inflicted on the *white* friends of the flying slave, still greater severities have been meted out towards the *coloured* man who was touched by tender sympathy for his race. In the same state of Delaware, about the same year, a worthy citizen of Wilmington, a free coloured man, named Samuel D. Burns, was convicted of the offence of aiding

slaves to escape; he was sentenced to pay a fine of 500
dollars and costs, to be imprisoned ten months, and
then sold to the highest bidder as a slave for fourteen
years. This sentence was of course equivalent to
selling him into life-long slavery; for who could find
him at the extreme South at the end of fourteen years,
or take sufficient interest in him to procure his freedom? This is only one of many such cases which have
come before the public; but who can tell how many,
without even a mock trial, without even a warning,
have been hurried off into life-long slavery, from
parents, husband, wife, and children, only for loving
their poor neighbour and helping him.

In 1849 occurred the case of Richard Dillingham,
which is one of peculiarly touching interest. He was
the son of most respectable Quaker parents in Ohio.
He was brought up by his pious mother in the doctrine of love to all mankind, and so in early manhood
he was found teaching the coloured people in Cincinnati and visiting the prisons. Some of his poor friends
in that city had relatives who were slaves in the State
of Tennessee. Richard's sympathies were so much
awakened, that he went into Tennessee to try what
could be done to effect a reunion among them. He was
detected in the act of paying the toll for a hack-car-
riage containing three coloured persons, and he, with
the three tenants of the carriage and the driver, were
arrested. He was put into jail in company with six
profane rude men, whose swearing and licentious talk
greatly grieved the pure mind of the young Christian;
and his hardships of other kinds were not trivial. His

G

letters at this time indicate his character more than
any description.   To his parents and brother he says,
" I have no hopes of getting clear of being convicted
and sentenced to the penitentiary, but do not think
that I am without comfort in my affliction, for I assure
you that I have many reflections that give me sweet
consolation in the midst of my grief.   I have a clear
conscience before my God, which is my greatest comfort and support through all my troubles and afflictions.
The greatest affliction I have is the reflection of the
sorrow and anxiety my friends will have to endure on
my account.   But I can assure thee, brother, that with
the exception of this reflection, I am far, very far, from
being one of the most miserable of men.   My hopes are
not fixed on this world, and therefore I have a source
of consolation that will never fail me, so long as I slight
not the offers of mercy, comfort, and peace, with which
my blessed Saviour constantly privileges me.   If it be
my fate to go to the penitentiary for eight or ten years,
I can, I believe, meet my doom without shedding a
tear. . . . I will not flinch from what I believe to be
right and honourable.   There was a time at my arrest
that I might in all probability have escaped the police,
but it would have subjected those who were arrested
with me to punishment, perhaps even to death, in order
to find out who I was; and if they had not told more
than they could have done in truth, they would probably have been punished without mercy; and I am
determined no one shall suffer for me.   I am now a
prisoner, but those who were arrested with me are all
at liberty, and I believe without whipping.   I now

stand alone before the commonwealth of Tennessee, to
answer for the affair. Tell my friends I am in the
midst of consolation here."

There are other letters of a still more touching
character addressed to an amiable young lady, of high
mental endowments, to whom he was engaged; in one
of these he says, " Oh, dearest, canst thou upbraid
me? canst thou call it a crime? Wouldst thou call it
a crime, or couldst thou upbraid me for rescuing, or
attempting to rescue, *thy* father, mother, or brother,
and sister, or even friends, from a captivity among a
cruel race of oppressors? Oh, couldst thou only see
what I have seen, and hear what I have heard of the
sad, vexatious, degrading, and soul-trying situation of
as noble souls as ever the Anglo-Saxon race were possessed of, mourning in vain for that universal heaven-
born boon of freedom which an all-wise and beneficent
Creator has designed for all, thou couldst not censure,
but wouldst deeply sympathize with me. . . . I have
happy hours here, and I should not be miserable if I
could only know you were not sorrowing for me at
home. It would give me more satisfaction to hear
that you were not grieving about me, than anything
else. The nearer I live to the principle of the commandment, ' Love thy neighbour as thyself,' the more
enjoyment I have of this life. None can know the
enjoyments that flow from feelings of goodwill towards
our fellow-beings but those who cultivate them. Even
in my prison cell I may be happy if I will; for the
Christian's consolation cannot be shut out from him
by enemies or iron gates. Though persecutions ever

G G

so severe be my lot, yet I will not allow my indignation ever to ripen into revenge even against my bitterest enemies; for there will be a time when all things
must be revealed before Him who has said, ' Vengeance is mine, I will repay.' . . . " Think not, however, that in my sad case all is loss to me, for by my
calamity I have learned many good and useful lessons,
which I hope may yet prove both temporal and spiritual blessings to me.

> ' Behind a frowning Providence
> He hides a smiling face.'

Therefore I hope thou and my dear distressed parents
will be somewhat comforted about me, for I know you
regard my spiritual welfare far more than anything
else." His next letter tells his friend that he has had
a severe moral conflict because of some methods of
escape being offered which he did not think of an
honourable character, and which he therefore declined.
He adds, " Thou need not fear that I shall ever stoop
to dishonourable means to avoid my severe impending
fate. When I meet thee again, I want to meet thee
with a clear conscience and a character unspotted by
disgrace."

To his parents he says :—" The principles of love to
my fellow-beings which you have instilled into my
mind are some of the greatest consolations I have in
my imprisonment; and they give me resignation to
bear whatever may be inflicted upon me, without feeling any malice or bitterness towards my persecutors.
I will endeavour to bear what they may inflict with
Christian fortitude and resignation, and try not to

murmur at my lot; but it is hard to obey the commandment, ' Love your enemies.' "

Such was the unvarying tone of his letters, affording a distinct echo of the sublime utterances of the martyred Saviour and the martyred Stephen eighteen hundred years before, " Father, forgive them, for they know not what they do;" " Lord, lay not this sin to their charge."

The day of trial of this young disciple came at length; his mother and her brother, Asa Williams, had travelled 750 miles to attend it; his mother sat by his side. After the speeches of the counsel in his defence had closed, Richard rose and made for himself a touching plea, which, with his youth, engaging manners, and unvarying gentleness, produced an impression even on that jury of slaveholders. He said he knew he had violated their laws, but he had done it from feelings of humanity. He was particularly anxious to exonerate every one from participation in his attempt, " for I alone am guilty; I alone committed the offence, and I alone must suffer the penalty. My parents, my friends, my relatives, are as innocent of any participation in or knowledge of my offence as the babe unborn. My parents are still living, though advanced in years, and in the course of nature a few more will terminate their earthly existence. In their old age and infirmity they will need a stay and protection; and if you can make my term of imprisonment a short one, you will receive the gratitude of a son who reverences his parents, and the prayers and blessings of an aged father and mother who love their child."

The jury retired and returned with a verdict for
three years' imprisonment in the penitentiary—the
shortest time allowed by the law for such an offence.
He was at first put to sawing and scrubbing stone, but
he was too delicate in frame for such labours; and as
he won upon the esteem of his jailors, he was promoted
to a more congenial situation as steward of the prison
hospital. He announced the change in a letter to his
friend, expressing his sense of responsibility in his new
office, and adds, " but I will try to do the best I can.
. . . I enjoy the comfort of a warm room and good fire,
and am allowed to sit up in the evenings and read,
which is a great privilege. . . . I have now been here
nine months, and have twenty-seven more to stay. It
seems to me a long time in prospect. I try to be as
patient as I can, but I sometimes get low-spirited.
What wounds my feelings most is the reflection of what
you all suffer of grief and anxiety for me. . . . As ever,
thine in the bonds of affection, R. D."

The release was nearer at hand than he thought. He
had been little more than a year in prison when the
cholera broke out among its inmates. Richard was indefatigable in his attendance on the sick people, day
and night. His delicate constitution, already weak-
ened by confinement, sank under the fresh pressure;
and this humble follower of his Lord laid down his
wearied life, and his spirit entered the realms of joy
and peace and love. Such was another of the martyrs
of this nineteenth century of Christianity in the United
States of America !

The poet Whittier wrote, in reference to his death,

a few lines which we may be pardoned for inserting here :—

" *Si crucem libenter portes, te portabit.*"—IMIT. CHRIST.

" ' THE cross, if freely borne, shall be
No burthen, but support to thee.'
So, moved of old time, for our sake
The holy man of Kempen spake.

Thou brave and true one, upon whom
Was laid the cross of martyrdom,
How didst thou in thy faithful youth
Bear witness to this blessed truth.

Thy cross of suffering and of shame
A staff within thy hands became,
In paths where faith alone could see
Thy Master's steps upholding thee.

Thine was the seed-time ; God alone
Beholds the end of what is sown;
Beyond our vision weak and dim,
The harvest-time is hid with him.

Yet unforgotten where it lies,
That seed of generous sacrifice,
Though seeming on the desert cast,
Shall rise with bloom and fruit at last."

CHAPTER VII.

THE year 1850 was signalised by the passing of that
series of compromise measures called " Clay's Omnibus
Bill."   This bill included within its provisions a clause
ceding to Texas 25,000 square miles of country for
slave territory, and granting to her ten millions of dollars as compensation for territory north of the boundary
line, to which without a shadow of right she had laid
claim.   Other clauses provided for the admission of
New Mexico and Utah into the Union, without any
mention of slavery in their constitution,—for the exclusion of slavery from California,—for the abolition of
the slave-trade in the District of Columbia,—and lastly,
for the infamous Fugitive Slave Law.   Such was this
remarkable bill, which was intended to set at rest
for ever the agitation of slavery in the United States.
Of all these provisions, the only two that claimed to be
anti-slavery were the admission of California as a free
state and the abolition of the slave-trade in the District
of Columbia, the twelve miles square in which the national capital was situated; the latter measure merely
meant the removal of the *slave market* to Alexandria,
just beyond the boundary line, while at the same time

it was expressly understood that with *slavery itself* in the District, Congress was pledged not to interfere. And although the Constitution gave Congress exclusive control there, it did not interfere till the year 1862, when the Union being severed, President Lincoln granted this measure of justice by proclaiming emancipation; offering, however, compensation to slaveholders for possible loss to the extent of 6,000,000 dollars.

All the other clauses of this " Omnibus Bill" were servile sops to slavery; but chief in iniquity was the Fugitive Slave Law. To Henry Clay and Daniel Webster belongs the infamy of carrying out this atrocious bill, whose provisions were arranged by Mason of Virginia (the recently appointed commissioner of the slave states to England); and Millard Filmore, who came into office by the death of President Taylor, promptly, by his signature, made it the law of the land. Great indignation was at first expressed throughout the Northern States, but after a time politicians, and sadder still, ministers of all denominations were found boldly to defend the law, and to advocate its being obeyed in defiance of the higher law of God. We give one or two quotations from the published sermons of these ministers of religion, which may tend to show that the American Church came forward once more to prove herself the " bulwark of American slavery."

The Rev. Dr. Gardiner Spring, an eminent Presbyterian clergyman of New York, well known in this country by his religious publications, declared from the pulpit that " if by one prayer he could liberate every slave in the United States, he would not dare to offer it."

The Rev. Dr. Joel Parker of· Philadelphia, in the course of a discussion on the nature of slavery, says, " What then are the evils inseparable from slavery? There is not one that is not equally inseparable from depraved human nature in other lawful relations."

The Rev. Moses Stuart, D.D. (late Professor in the Theological College, Andover), in his vindication of this bill, reminds his readers that " many Southern slaveholders are true *Christians.*" That " sending back a fugitive to them is not like restoring one to an idolatrous people." That " though we may *pity* the fugitive, yet the Mosaic law does not authorise the rejection of the claims of the slaveholders to their stolen or strayed *property.*" This great theologian quite forgot Deut. xiii. 15, 16.

The Rev. W. M. Rogers, an orthodox minister of Boston, delivered on Thanksgiving-day a sermon, in which he says, " When the slave asks me to stand between him and his master, what does he ask? He asks me to murder a nation's life; and I will not do it, because I have a conscience—because there is a God." He proceeds to affirm, that if this resistance to the carrying out of the " Fugitive Slave Law" should lead the magistracy to call the citizens to arms, their duty was to obey, and " if ordered to take human life, in the name of God to take it;" and he concludes by admonishing the fugitives to " hearken to the word of God, and to count their own masters worthy of all honour."

The Rev. Dr. Taylor, an Episcopal clergyman of New Haven, Connecticut, made a speech at a Union meeting, in which he deprecates the agitation on the new law and urges obedience to it, asking, " Is that article in the Constitution contrary to the law of nature, of nations, or to the will of God : Is it so ? Is there a shadow of reason for saying it ? I have not been able to discover it. Have I not shown you it is lawful to deliver up, in compliance with their laws, fugitive slaves, for the high, the great, the momentous interests of those [Southern] states."

The Right Rev. Bishop Hopkins of Vermont, in a lecture at Lockport, on the 13th January 1850, while admitting that slavery, from its *inherent nature*, had in every age been a curse and a blight to the nation which cherished it, throws the sacred mantle of the Scriptures over it. He says, " It was warranted by the Old Testament;" and inquires, " What effect had the gospel in doing away with slavery ? None whatever." Therefore he argues, as it is expressly permitted by the Bible, it does not in itself involve any sin; but that every Christian is authorised by the divine law to own slaves, provided they were not treated with unnecessary cruelty.

The Rev. Orville Dewey, D. D., of the Unitarian connection, maintains in his lectures that the safety of the Union is not to be hazarded for the sake of the African race. He declares that, for his part, he would send his own brother or child into slavery, if needed to preserve the union between the free and slaveholding states ; and counsels the slave to similar magnanimity.

While such were the sentiments of these and the generality of the professed Christian ministers of the free states, we rejoice to have on record many noble sentiments of the truly Christian minority, which time and space forbid our quoting.

Although the constitutional provisions had enabled slaveholders to claim their property since the establishment of the nation, the Fugitive Slave Law gave a new stimulus to the horrid trade of man-hunting, by *requiring* Northern citizens, under penalty of *fine at least*, to assist in the crime of rendition, and many a poor man was hurried from the useful toil by which he was maintaining a free wife and children, to be tried and sentenced back to slavery. Many a poor woman who was living honourably with the husband of her choice in fancied security, suddenly found herself seized, proved to be a slave, and sent back to slavery; and with all her children, for, unless it could be proved that they were born in a free state, their condition followed hers.

The narratives of that period are of a most heart-rending description. The case of William and Ellen Craft may be familiar to many of our readers, but it is a very good illustration. Their daring escape from slavery, in the first instance, is one of thrilling interest. They thought their dangers and anxieties were over when they reached Boston, where William pursued his trade as a carpenter and Ellen by her needle aided in maintaining their little home in comfort, and the expected birth of a free baby made their freedom the sweeter, when, like a thunder-bolt, came the Fugitive

Slave Law, scattering terror and dismay. They dared
not be seen in the streets, and William provided arms
to protect himself and his wife ; but there was no security when they knew the warrant was out against
them. By the aid of abolitionists, through extreme
peril, they were put on board a vessel bound for Liver-
pool and landed in England safe and *really free.*

But not many cases have had such a happy issue.
No coloured man or woman was safe in the whole
United States, and many who were even by state
laws born *free* were kidnapped and enslaved. Terror
reigned, and whole families, and the larger portion of
coloured churches, set out under cover of night in the
cold winter of 1850–51 to seek the protection of Queen
Victoria in Canada, where their sufferings from the
climate and inadequate provision were very great.
The abolitionists had work enough now on their hands,
to warn the fugitives of danger, to aid them to escape,
to defend them in court if brought to trial, to stand
by them in every circumstance, and to share their trials
by sympathy and fellow-suffering. Some of these sufferings were neither light nor trivial.

In the month of August 1850, in the city of Washington, William L. Chaplin, a gentleman of high respectability and long-tried devotion to the cause of the
slave, attempted to assist five of his brethren to escape,
by affording them places in his carriage. The design
became known, the carriage was stopped, the fugitives
were carried back to bondage, and W. L. Chaplin was
violently arrested and lodged in the jail at Washington. Ultimately he was remanded to imprisonment

in Maryland, as in that state his offence would, on his trial, be most likely to be visited with rigorous severity. False indictments were multiplied against him, and bail laid at 19,000 dollars, which must be deposited with the courts before he could breathe the free air. After being imprisoned for many months, bail was found and he was released.

A very remarkable case occurred on the 11th of September 1851. Early on that morning a party of slave-hunters was discovered lying in wait for their prey near the house of William Parker, in the neighbourhood of Christiana, Lancaster county, Pennsylvania. When discovered and challenged, they demanded the slave. Parker assured them he was not there. The assailants attempted to enforce a search, and fired two shots into the house. Parker then gave the alarm by blowing a horn, and the neighbourhood was raised. Thirty or fifty coloured men were soon on the ground, most of them partially armed. Castnor Hanway and Elijah Lewis, both of them white men, and members of the Society of Friends, rode up before the engagement began and endeavoured to persuade the slaveholders to withdraw. The deputy-marshal ordered them to join the posse, which of course they refused to do. Gorsuch, the slaveholder, and his son, and their party, persisted in their attempt to capture the negroes by force, and fired on the coloured men, who returned the fire with fatal effect. Gorsuch was killed on the spot, his son severely but not mortally wounded, and the party was put to flight. The dead and wounded were cared for by the Friends and the neighbours, who were mostly abolitionists, and the slave who was the object of pursuit escaped to freedom and safety.

When news spread of this adventure, great was the excitement; Judge Grier in open court denounced the act of the coloured people as coming under the charge of high treason, and an order was given to arrest, on this grave charge, all engaged in resisting the execution of the Fugitive Slave Law. Thirty persons, coloured and white, were accordingly seized and lodged in jail to await their trial. The white men arrested were Castnor Hanway and Elijah Lewis, who came to the scene as peacemakers, and took no other part than to risk their lives in attempting to withdraw the assailants, and, after the mélée, to protect the dead and succour the wounded. Nevertheless they were charged with high treason, and brought to trial on the 24th of November. Even Judge Grier then saw that the charge against these men could not be sustained with any show of decency, and the jury acquitted them. The coloured men were also discharged, after the party had been kept four months in strict imprisonment, suffering greatly from bad ventilation and a deficiency of the common necessaries of life.

The next case which excited popular interest was that of Jerry at Syracuse. In this case also a rescue was effected, but without loss of life or effusion of blood. Nevertheless, the men who had determinedly interposed to save their brother from slavery were most rigorously prosecuted by the United States Government, while Jerry became a British subject in Canada.

Another case in 1851 deserves a passing notice. The Fugitive Slave Law, as we have already said, not only seized those who had once been slaves, but very frequently kidnapped those who were born *free* by the laws of the States. Many were the cases of this kind which came to the knowledge of the slaves' friends; but many, many more there were from whom no message was sent to tell of the agony of the moment of seizure, when the conviction dawned on the poor victim that he was to be a slave for life.

On December 30, 1851, Rachel Parker was taken from the house of Joseph C. Miller of Chester county, Pennsylvania, by two rough men, at the instance of Thomas M'Creary, Maryland. Joseph Miller was not present when Rachel was seized, but was hastily called by Mrs. Miller. He tried to stop the men; they swore that Rachel Parker was the slave of a Mr. Schoolfield in Baltimore. This was an audacious falsehood, as Rachel and her sister (who had been carried away before) were well known to be free. After being long detained in jail, these two young women, more happy than most in such circumstances, were liberated; but the part of this story which more particularly concerns this narrative, is the fate of poor Mr. Miller. Finding he could not prevent the girl being taken away, he followed her to Baltimore, in order to give his evidence on her behalf. He made a charge of kidnapping against M'Creary, and while it was pending he and his friends returned homewards by railway. On the arrival of the train at the terminus he was missing, and search being made, not far from one of the intermediate stations he was found suspended from a tree: it was believed that the hatred of the slaveholder, or his desire to get rid of the most troublesome witness, had induced this terrible deed, but no steps were ever taken to punish the kidnappers, or to detect the murderers of poor Miller.

Another case in Pennsylvania was that of Daniel Kauffman; against him and several others an action was brought for the offence of concealing and harbouring slaves—the sum of which offence was, that a night's lodging and food had been supplied to a party of fugitives in Kauffman's barn. Judge Grier charged the jury with his wonted violence and indecency of language, and although the evidence was insufficient to prove that Kauffman knew the party to be fugitive slaves, he was convicted and assessed with damages at 2800 dollars, being more than the entire amount of his property.

These are a few specimens of the sufferings of those who befriended the fugitive slaves during the first year after the passing of the bill. On the whole, although productive of an immense amount of misery, the measure was, in regard to the rendition of slaves, a failure; the number returned was comparatively small and the cost enormous, while the escapes were very numerous.

The Fugitive Slave Law, in fact, served as a perpetual cause of agitation on every fresh attempt to enforce it. The case of Anthony Burns, who was arrested at Boston on the 24th of May 1854, and carried off to slavery on the 2nd of June, was remarkably exciting.

H

There were circumstances of peculiar importance and
interest connected with this case; one of which was,
that a petition for the repeal of the law was sent to
Congress, signed by four thousand of the leading merchants of Boston, none of them hitherto identified with
anti-slavery. Another incident was the resignation of
office by Joseph K. Hayes, captain of the watch and
police, who preferred to relinquish his position rather
than be implicated in the execution of the infamous
Fugitive Slave Bill. A large meeting of influential
gentlemen took place on the 26th of June to do
honour to Mr. Hayes, and to present to him a testi-
monial of appreciation of his righteous act.

The rendition of Burns occurring in Boston was
well calculated to dishearten the abolitionists; but even
then, at the very period of their city's degradation,
they tell us that they could yet take courage. " The
noonday effulgence," they say, " is approaching; God's
word and government and existence are pledged for it;
it is not in the power of man or of combined governments to prevent it. We are thankful that we can not
only see, but feel it too, and show it to others in this
hour of our temporary defeat, calamity, and sorrow."
About the same time the veteran J. R. Giddings, in
the House of Representatives, after a scathing review
of the President's message, which had avoided all allu-
sion to the important subject of slavery, concluded as
follows :—" The question of lending our support to
slavery is presented in too many forms and shapes to
be avoided. The great heart of the nation throbs for
a total separation from the contagion of slavery. To

this result the popular tide is setting and rolling with a force which no human arm can withstand. It will overwhelm all who oppose it. Let the lovers of justice, those who fear God and regard mankind, lift up their heads and rejoice, the day of our country's redemption draws nigh. Christianity, in its progress, is unfolding to public gaze the crimes of oppression. Those who 'frame wickedness by law' are fleeing before the popular indignation; they cannot endure its fervent heat. This work will continue to progress until the opponents of liberty shall be driven from our United States, and the North shall become disenthralled from the contagion of human bondage."

And now another influence which the Fugitive Slave Law had called into life sprung forth and spread with unparalleled effect. We allude to the publication of "Uncle Tom's Cabin," by Mrs. Harriet Beecher Stowe; its power was instantly felt, and it is unnecessary to remind our readers of the wonderfully rapid diffusion of that marvellous book. Mrs. Stowe herself says in respect to it, "I can only see that when a higher Being has purposes to accomplish, he can make a grain of mustard seed the means. I wrote what I did, because as a woman, as a mother, I was oppressed and heartbroken with the sorrows and injustice I saw; because, as a Christian, I felt the dishonour of Christianity; because, as a lover of my country, I trembled at the coming day of wrath. It is no merit in the sorrowful that they weep, nor to the oppressed that they gasp and struggle, nor to me that I must speak for those who cannot speak for themselves." The publication of

H H

the " Key " just after that of " Uncle Tom's Cabin," completed this great effort for the benefit of the cause, which did more to awaken the attention of the world to the wrongs of the slave than any other individual agency could have done, and proclaimed an exulting defiance to the reiterated declarations of Congress, that the agitation of the slavery question must cease.

CHAPTER VIII.

POSITION OF THE COLOURED PEOPLE.—BARRIERS TO THEIR EDUCATION.
—MISS MINER AT WASHINGTON.—MRS. MARGARET DOUGLAS AND
HER DAUGHTER ROSA, IN VIRGINIA.—NATIONAL SCHOOLS OPENED
TO COLOURED CHILDREN IN BOSTON IN 1855.—REPUDIATION OF
THE MISSOURI COMPROMISE, MARCH 4TH, 1854.—KANSAS.—STATE
RIGHTS AFFECTED.—PASSMORE WILLIAMSON IN THE CASE OF JANE
JOHNSON.—MARGARET GARNER.—1856. — INCREASED ATROCITIES
IN THE SOUTH.—JOHN C. UNDERWOOD.—REV. EDWARD MATTHEWS.
—REV. JESSE M'BRIDE.

THE loss of caste sustained by those in the Northern
States who associated on friendly terms with the free
people of colour has been alluded to as a frequent
cause of suffering; and very severe in some cases were
the penalties to those who taught the coloured people
to read the Bible.

The case of Miss Prudence Crandall, in the early
days of anti-slavery effort, cannot have been forgotten,
and we have now to mention one or two kindred cases
which occurred about this time. One of these, that of
Miss Miner, is thus described by Mrs H. B. Stowe in
1853 :—" Miss Miner has been for many years a heroic
and most indefatigable labourer for the coloured people
at Washington. She has been gifted by nature with
singular talents for this work, and endowed by God's
grace with a courage, zeal, and devotion such as are
given to but few. When her school was yet in its
infancy, it excited bitter opposition. A man one day
called upon her and told her that a mob was organised
to destroy her school-room, as they were determined

that her school should no longer exist. ' What good will it do to destroy my school-room ?' was her reply; ' I shall only get another and go right on.' ' But,' said he, ' we will frighten your scholars so that they will not dare to come to you.' ' No, you will not,' said she. ' Wherever I dare to go to teach, they will dare to come to learn.' Then fixing her eyes very decidedly on the man, she added, ' You may tell your associates that destroying any number of school-houses will not stop my school; you cannot stop it unless you take my life.' The man retired, and the school-room remained unmolested. This school has exerted a great influence on the minds of many slaveholders, who on visiting it have been struck with the capabilities, under education, of the very people whom they hold in slavery." In defiance of very great trials and difficulties, the school thus continued for many years, and Mrs. Stowe appropriated to its support 1000 dollars of the " Penny Offering " Fund.

The next case of this kind, to which we may advert, is that of Mrs. Margaret Douglas of Norfolk, Virginia, in the year 1853. She was a respectable widow lady, who with her daughter had settled there from South Carolina, and they were quietly and honourably maintaining themselves and doing deeds of charity. About the end of the year 1851 Mrs. Douglas met with some intelligent little coloured children who were earnestly desirous of learning to read. She offered the services of her daughter to help them, and after a time, finding they made great progress, it was decided to open a regular school for little coloured children. This was an

entirely satisfactory undertaking, and for nearly a year
the little ones came with great pleasure to learn to
read and write, and showed very great aptitude.   But
it was not to continue.   On the 9th of May 1853,
under the authority of the mayor, constables were sent
to arrest Mrs. Douglas, her daughter, and their eighteen
or twenty little coloured scholars.   The latter were
dispersed, and Mrs. Douglas and her daughter were remanded for examination.   Mrs. Douglas was quite
ignorant of the laws of the State which prohibited the
teaching of free coloured children, nevertheless she was
summoned for trial, and after pleading in her own
defence with an ability and dignity very unexpected
by the prosecuting party, she was sentenced to one
month's imprisonment; the sufferings and privations
connected with which were not bounded by the length
of her sentence.

This case occurred almost contemporaneously with
the analogous ones of the Madiai and Miss Cunningham
in Tuscany, which excited the indignation of Christen-
dom, and America was not behind the rest of the world
in condemning the despotic tyranny of the Grand
Duke, while deeds such as we have recorded were
enacted without rebuke on her own soil, and by the
magistrates of her own states.

This subject of the education of coloured children
was from very early days an interesting one to the
abolitionists. As their experience advanced, they found
that to have *separate coloured schools* in the free states
promoted the caste and prejudice which were so inju-
rious to this oppressed people, so their efforts were

directed towards obtaining admission for those children
into the common schools which all alike were taxed to
support; and surely in our record of the sufferers of
this period we must not omit the dear little children
sent by their parents to school to uphold the principle
of equal rights irrespective of colour, which they did with
a heroism beyond their years. In Philadelphia the children of Mr. Robert Purvis, a gentleman of education,
respectability, and wealth, who paid his full share to
support the schools, were sent home time after time
weeping to their mother, having been turned out of the
school because they had a tinge of African blood in
their veins. In Boston Sarah Parker Remond, a lady
well known in this country for her intelligence and the
powerful eloquence with which she has pleaded for her
sisters in bonds, was sent by her parents with her brother and sisters to the common schools; they were frequently expelled, and on one occasion Sarah received
considerable injury from the rudeness with which she
was treated. In Boston, at least, these efforts were not
without eventual success, although the struggle was
somewhat protracted.

In 1840 William Lloyd Garrison, Wendell Phillips,
Francis Jackson, Henry W. Williams, and William C.
Nell, petitioned the legislature to open the free schools
in Boston to children of all classes, without respect of
colour. The petition was thrown aside contemptuously,
but the petitioners were not men to be daunted; they
kept their claims before the public. In 1846 another
petition, signed by 86, was forwarded; in 1849, one
signed by 228; and so the interest proceeded, till by

decree of legislature, on the 3d of September 1855, the
public schools were thrown open, and many were the
manifestations among the coloured people of gratitude
for the boon, and appreciation of its importance. One
little boy, passing the exclusive school where he had
previously been a pupil, exclaimed, " Good bye, coloured school! to-morrow we are like other Boston
boys." This interesting event was signalized by a
public meeting in honour of William C. Nell, himself a
man of colour, who had been the principal agent in
securing this measure of justice to his race.

The extension of the right of suffrage to the people
of colour was a point strongly urged by many of their
friends, but as yet this privilege is not generally accorded. In most of the New England states, and some
parts of Ohio, they have the franchise without any
other conditions than those applicable to white men;
and in the state of New York the possession of real
estate to the value of 250 dollars qualifies a coloured
man to vote, while in the other free states they are
excluded from nearly all social and political rights.
Everywhere injustice has prevailed; and even since the
terrible war began, this monstrous prejudice for a long
time prevented the Federal Government accepting the
services of coloured volunteers.

In 1853 and 1854 the principal subject which agitated the Congressional debates, and the whole country,
was the Kansas Nebraska Bill, by which, in shameless
violation of faith, and in repudiation of the Missouri
compromise, an attempt was made to create two slave
states out of lands solemnly consecrated to liberty.

The bill passed in the senate on the 4th of March 1854, by a vote of 2 to 14; it did not pass without resistance, and great efforts were made to arrest the infamy. Among the most able speakers on this occasion were Mr. Seward of New York and Charles Sumner of Massachusetts. On the 15th of May the bill passed the House of Representatives by 113 to 100. It then received the sanction of President Pierce, and this vast domain was opened to slavery, when its population should reach the number necessary for its formation into states, and its admission to the Union. The Northern feeling was aroused against this outrage, and prompted a determination to secure, by extensive emigration of free settlers, a preponderance of the friends of freedom in the new territory. Missouri poured in hordes of slaveholders and unprincipled ruffians to defeat this determination, and a terrible struggle ensued at the ballot-box and in the field, and martyrs to the cause of freedom in America were multiplied daily; men, women, and children suffered terribly from assaults, robberies, loss of house and home, starvation, and the murder of dear friends. We have already alluded to this struggle, and it is not necessary to enter into its details, as they are easily accessible in connexion with the life of John Brown of Ossawatomie and Harper's Ferry.* But these struggles were not in vain. They resulted in freedom to Kansas; they strengthened the cause of Liberty in the United States; they called into vigour the Republican

---

* "Life and Letters of Captain John Brown," edited by Richard D. Webb. Smith, Elder, & Co., 65 Cornhill, London.

anti-slavery political party; and sent forth John Brown to proclaim emancipation at Harper's Ferry.

In 1855 occurred a very interesting case, which affected the interpretation of the free state laws in respect to slavery. On the 18th of July of that year a slaveholder of the name of Wheeler was passing through Philadelphia as accredited minister from Washington to Nicaragua. He had with him his slave Jane Johnson and her two sons, Daniel and Isaiah, aged respectively about seven and twelve years. By a law of Pennsylvania, all slaves brought into the state by their masters become *free*. Jane Johnson had told two of the coloured servants at the hotel that she wished very much to have her liberty. This was reported to William Still, the Secretary of the Vigilance Committee, and to Passmore Williamson, the Secretary of the Old Abolition Society, originated in 1789 for the express protection of negroes unlawfully held in bondage. These men were prompt and wise in the performance of their duty; they hastened to the hotel and found that Wheeler and his slave had left for the steamer at the wharf. Thither Passmore Williamson followed them, and at once spoke to Jane Johnson, who was seated on deck; and in the presence of Wheeler he told her if she wished to be free she had nothing to do but walk on shore, for by the laws of the state she was already free. After a few minutes of bewildered hesitation, during which Mr. Williamson and Mr. Still repeated the announcement, and Mr. Wheeler did all he could to dissuade Jane from leaving him, she rose and took one of the children by the hand. Wheeler seized her and held her fast to her seat, till Mr. Williamson interposed, assisted her to rise, and restrained Wheeler till she had reached the ladder leading from the steamer. Her two children were carried after her, and the party were immediately placed in a carriage, and, amidst the cheers of the people, were driven to a place of safety. For his agency in this matter Passmore Williamson was served with a writ of *habeas corpus*, commanding him to produce the three slaves at the instance of "their owner," John H. Wheeler. This was the only issue on which the slaveholder could act, as it was clearly not a case under the Fugitive Slave Law, since he himself had brought his slaves into the state. To the disgrace of Judge Kane of the United States District Court, he granted the writ, thereby conceding the right of the slaveholder, and ignoring one of the best laws of his own state. Passmore Williamson courteously replied to the writ, that the three persons named were not now nor ever had been in his custody, and had never been restrained in their liberty by him, so that he could not produce their bodies in court. Judge Kane would not admit this explanation, and on the 27th committed the prisoner Passmore Williamson for contempt of court, *without bail or mainprize;* and he remained in Moyamensing prison during three months of a hot summer, suffering in health and estate from this forcible detention from business and family claims. He made an attempt to procure his liberation by an appeal to Judge Lewis of the Supreme Court of Pennsylvania, but in vain. Judge Lewis sustained the decision of Judge Kane, as did also the full bench of the Supreme Court with one exception—Justice Knox, who maintained the true character of *habeas corpus,* and that the prisoner was entitled to its protection. In regard to the matter of the original charge, he declared, " That when the owner of a slave voluntarily brings his slave from a slave to a free state, without any intention of remaining therein, the right of the slave to his freedom depends upon the law of the state to which he is brought. That if a slave is brought into a free state and escapes from the custody of his master while in said state, the right of the master to reclaim him is not a question arising under the constitution of the United States or the laws thereof, and therefore a judge of the United States cannot issue a writ of *habeas corpus* directed to one who it is alleged withholds the possession of the slave from his master, commanding him to produce the body of the slave before the said judge."

The next effort was made at the instance of Jane Johnson, who petitioned for the liberation of Passmore Williamson, stating the whole case, to the facts of which she made oath before a magistrate in Boston; but Judge Kane decided that she had no *status* in court, and so her petition could not be received. Judge Kane was, however, becoming a little tired of his unenviable notoriety as the upholder of the slaveholder's interest in defiance of a state law, and as the persccutor of a highly respected citizen of Philadelphia for maintaining that law, so he consented to receive an application from Mr. Williamson to relieve him from the charge of contempt of court; and although the state-

ments were substantially the same as he made in reply to the original writ, he was discharged.   We have
given this case to show how disgracefully subservient
the judges of the free states had become to the slaveholding interest.

A year later this subserviency was announced in a
still more decided manner.   The case of the Garner
family demonstrated another conflict between pro-
slavery United States law and state sovereignty.   On
the 27th of January 1855, Simon Garner and his wife,
with their son Robert and his wife Margaret, and four
of their children, attempted to escape from Kentucky.
They crossed the Ohio river on the ice, and took
refuge at the house of a free coloured man named
Kite, near Cincinnati.   They were tracked, and with
the necessary warrants from the United States' commissioners, the slaveholder came to seize his slaves.
Considerable resistance was made ineffectually, and
on entering the house the slaveholder proceeded to
claim his property; but in one case, at least, another
claimant had been before him.   Margaret Garner had
formed the firm determination to secure her children's
freedom.   All other means had failed her, so she sought
the help of an agent who is no respecter of persons,
and with her own hand attempted to release by *death*
the spirits of her four children.   She had succeeded in
the case of one little girl, whom the hunters found
dead.   This is a terrible story, and speaks loudly of
what the miseries and degradation of slavery must be,
when a mother chose the fearful alternative of taking
the lives of her children with her own hands rather

than that they should return to slavery. As this murder took place in Ohio, Margaret Garner and her husband and parents were amenable to the law of that state on the charge of murder, and•of being accessory thereto; but though the fugitives were detained at Cincinnati four weeks, they were merely tried as *fugitives from labour*, and delivered up to be carried south. If Ohio had promptly asserted her rights, these poor people would at least have had a chance for freedom. As it was, when, after much pressure, a writ was issued for their arrest, they were already far on their way to slavery, and the demand for their detention was utterly disregarded. To the boat which conveyed them, some little accident occurred, and Margaret either sprang or was thrown into the water, with her infant in her arms. She was taken up, but the child was washed away, and the mother was heard to rejoice, as the waters closed over it, that it also was *free*. This was the last that was heard of her and her two children, her husband and his parents. Probably they were sold and separated at the auction-block, and may still be suffering the horrors of slavery.

In 1856 the irrepressible conflict between slavery and freedom began to assume a more decided shape. The cases of atrocity in the South against free white citizens of the North suspected of abolitionism were multiplied; even yet the Northern states submitted, and no demand was made for reparation of injuries or satisfaction. A respectable citizen, John C. Underwood, was expelled from Virginia for expressing views

hostile to slavery. On the 14th of June, the Rev.
William Sellers, a minister of the Methodist Church
(North), suspected of abolitionism, was tarred and
feathered for attempting to preach at Rodustu, Missouri, and an aged and beloved member of that
church, Benjamin Holland, was murdered. A few
years before, the Rev. Edward Matthews of Wisconsin, an agent of the American Free Mission Baptist
Society, went, in his missionary vocation, to preach in
Kentucky. He expressed anti-slavery sympathies, and
applied for various public places in which to preach,
but in vain; he then held a meeting attended by free
coloured people, where he was assailed by a mob, who
drove him out of the village. He afterwards wrote an
account of the transaction, which he left at the office of
the Richmond *Chronicle*, from which he was turning
away, when he was seized by four men, and led to a
lonely place, where was a pond. They determined to
duck him, and having ascertained that he could swim,
threw him as far as they could into the pond, and told
him to come out. He did so; but refusing to promise
to leave Richmond, they threw him in again. This
was repeated six times, when he was almost quite
exhausted, and at length he gave the required pledge
and left the state. The Rev. Edward Matthews has
been in this country several years, and has faithfully
advocated the cause of the slave, exposed the short-
comings of the American Churches, and pointed out
the duty of all true Christians in regard to the oppressed. A few months previous to this outrage on a
respectable free white minister of the gospel, the Rev.

Jesse M'Bride of the Wesleyan Connection, from Ohio, was violently treated in North Carolina and expelled from the state. His offence seems to have been an attempt to gather a church of non-slaveholders. He had made an engagement to preach, and although very unwell, he determined to keep his engagement. He was warned that the mob was likely to interfere with him, and was requested to remain at home; but like John Bunyan of old, he was not to be thus deterred from trying to do his Master's will. He was prevented going to the platform, but knelt down outside of the enclosure and prayed for strength. Then he rose quite calm, and mildly replying to the taunts of the rioters, proceeded to give out a hymn. He then prayed fervently with the people, and notwithstanding the rudeness of some, he believes many could say, " It is good for us to be here." His own account of the transaction is very interesting and graphic; and in conclusion he says, " I am more and more confirmed in the righteousness of our cause. I would rather, much rather, die for good principles than have applause and honour for propagating false theories and abominations. You would perhaps like to know how I feel. Happy most of the time. A religion that will not stand persecution will not take us to heaven. Blessed be God that I have not thus far been suffered to deny him. Sometimes I have thought that I was nearly home. I generally feel a calmness of soul, but sometimes my enjoyments are rapturous. I have had a great burden of prayer for the dear flock. Help me to pray for them. Thank God I have not heard of one of them giving up

I

or turning; and I believe some, if not most of them, would go to the stake rather than give back. I forgot to say I read a part of the fifth chapter of the Acts of the Apostles to the rioters, beginning at the seventeenth verse. I told them if their institutions were of God I could not harm them; that if our cause was of God they could not stop it; that they could kill me, but they could not kill the truth. Though I talked plainly, I talked and felt kindly to them."

CHAPTER IX.

HON. CHARLES SUMNER.—REPUBLICAN PARTY.—ELECTION OF 1856.—
JOHN C. FREMONT.—PRESIDENT BUCHANAN.—SOUTHERN FURY.—
DRED SCOTT DECISION.—1857.—COMMERCIAL CRISIS.—REVIVALS.
—1858.—PROSCRIPTION OF FREE COLOURED PEOPLE IN MARYLAND,
VIRGINIA, AND ARKANSAS.—OBERLIN RESCUE CASE.—INTERESTING
FUGITIVE TRIAL AT PHILADELPHIA.

SUCH are some illustrations of the results of mob law
in the slave states. We have now to introduce a very
remarkable illustration of mob violence in the senate of
the United States; not the only one or by any means
the first which has taken place within the halls of
Congress, but one which excited extraordinary interest,
and has not been without its influence on the cause of
freedom in the nation. We allude to the outrage on
the Hon. Charles Sumner, senator for Massachusetts,
perpetrated by Preston L. Brooks, senator from South
Carolina. Charles Sumner is a native of Massachusetts, and an intimate friend of Wendell Phillips and
other abolitionists, though not exactly identified with
them in political principles or modes of operation. We
hear of him as early as the year 1846 refusing to lecture
to audiences from which coloured men were excluded,
and from time to time his name is incidentally mentioned in the history of current events, and always on
the side of the slave. He was elected senator for Massachusetts on the 24th of April 1851, and great was
the satisfaction that such a man should take the place
of Daniel Webster, whose death so soon after his shame-

I I

ful truckling to slavery in the matter of the fugitive
slave law had left a vacancy in the representation.

For some time, to the disappointment of many,
Charles Sumner's voice was not heard in the senate.
It was not till the 26th of August 1852 that he made
his remarkable speech against the constitutionality of
the fugitive slave law; and in the beginning of the following year he grew so troublesome to the slave power,
that he was not allowed to serve on committees.   Still
he went on giving his voice on the side of freedom, till
he became too formidable an opponent, and the Southerners and their allies sought some opportunity to
silence him.   On the 19th and 20th of May 1855,
according to his intention expressed to a friend in Boston, "to pronounce the most thorough philippic against
slavery ever uttered in a legislative body," he made
his celebrated speech on Kansas.   This was calculated
to rouse up all the animosity of his opponents, and they
made the occasion serve as a pretext to inflict on him
a characteristic response, not the response of argument
or eloquence, but that of the cowardly assassin.   For
two days a convenient opportunity was sought; and it
was on the 22nd, while he was busily engaged in writing at his desk, his head bent down over his paper,
and thoroughly unprepared for any assault, Senators
Brooks and Reitt, representatives of South Carolina,
approached him, and the former, without warning,
struck him several severe blows on the head with a
cane, which were repeated till he fell bleeding and
senseless on the floor of the senate-chamber.   Brooks
afterwards acknowledged that it was his intention to

kill the senator if he made any resistance. The assault
was witnessed with evident satisfaction, and without
the slightest interference, by Senators Douglas, Slidell,
and Toombs, all Southerners or in the slaveholding interest. Messrs. Murray and Morgan, from New York,
then came forward and rescued the helpless man from
the cowardly blows still being showered upon him.
Senator Sumner suffered for years from the effects of
this ruffianly attack, and it was at one time feared he
would never recover his vital energy; but the cause of
the slave had reason for gratitude in that he was at
length restored to his place in the senate, to all his former vigour, and even more than his former fervour on
the side of freedom. His speech on the " Barbarism of
Slavery," delivered since his restoration, is a wonderful epitome of the whole subject, and will well repay
perusal. He is instant in season and out of season,
bringing forward anti-slavery motions, and watching
over the interests of the slaves most faithfully. Instead
of the hearty denunciations and condemnation merited
by Brooks, he was feted and congratulated on the deed
he had done; presents of canes, silver and gold-headed,
without number, were given to him, and he at once
rose from obscurity to renown. But feeling in the
North was awakened more than by any previous outrage, and tended no doubt to stimulate the vigour
with which the Presidential election of 1856 was carried on.

The republican party started as a candidate John
C. Fremont, who, while he only went so far in politics as
to accept the republican " platform" for the non-exten-

sion of slavery, yet at heart was truly anti-slavery, as he has proved by the circumstances by which his name has become favourably known to the world since the breaking out of the present war in the United States. The loss of position from his effort to proclaim emancipation shows that he too had some degree of martyrdom to bear, like all others who in any way have sought to free the slaves. It is well known that the election of 1856 did not result in the appointment of a republican president; but once more a slaveholder at heart ruled in the United States, and James Buchanan signalised himself by his devotion to slavery.

Although the republican party was, as we have seen, of very diluted anti-slavery principles, yet it was a strong indication of the progress of opinion, and as such it was hailed by the abolitionists, while it excited the fear and rage of the slaveholding party. Adhesion to it or to Fremont was sure to provoke persecution and insult in the South, and many a luckless Northern man, for the simplest words used in conversation, was expelled from his Southern home without trial or jury, at a few hours' notice, and without being allowed time to collect his property. The irritability which vented itself in this way, causing much suffering to innocent victims, showed that the South trembled for the possession of its arbitrary power; but as yet anti-slavery sentiment at the North had not become strong enough to elect even a republican president. Shortly after the result of the election was made known, it was discovered that organised insurrectionary movements were preparing among the slaves of Tennessee; from

which it would seem that the slaves had been hoping
that their liberty would be gained by the election of an
anti-slavery president. When Fremont was rejected,
the information spread among them with great rapidity,
and under feelings of intense disappointment, a plot
was formed to secure what they found they could not
expect from the chief magistrate of the nation. The
plot being discovered on the very eve of its execution,
measures were adopted to counteract it; vigilance committees, patrols, and spies were appointed; arrests were
made, torture of the most cruel description was used to
procure confession, Lynch law with its summary process finished the business, and scourging and hanging
were the order of the day. The slaveholders' terrors
magnified the extent of the combination, and of course
many innocent victims suffered. We hear of nineteen
negroes being hung within a few days at Dover, and
nine at Cumberland, Tennessee; of one man having
died after a terrible whipping to make him confess;
and of others having submitted to *five or six hundred
lashes* before they would or could give the information
the tyrants wished to obtain from them. Free coloured
and white men were also involved in these terrible in-
flictions. One at least of the former and two of the
latter were hung on bare suspicion of favouring the
slaves, and sufferings and oppressions were multiplied
in the slave states.

It was in this year, 1856, that that infamous piece
of judicial villany called the *Dred Scott decision* was
enacted. The facts from which it originated may be
very briefly summed up. Dred Scott had formerly

been a slave in Missouri. He was taken by his master into Illinois, and thence into the territory north of
that state, where slavery had been prohibited by act of
Congress. Afterwards, on being brought back into
Missouri, he claimed his freedom, on the plea that he
had been voluntarily taken by his master into a free
state, and that, having been pronounced free by the
state laws, he could not be re-enslaved on returning
to a slave state. The state court acknowledged the
validity of the claim, but a writ of error was served,
and the question was ultimately referred to the Supreme
Court of the United States. This is the highest judicial
tribunal in the land, and is composed of nine judges.
Four of them were from the slave states, slaveholders
or their friends, and five from the free states, who,
with two exceptions, Judges M'Lean and Curtis, sym-
pathised with slaveholders, so there could be little
chance for the slave who sought justice at their hands.
And yet even those who were familiar with the subserviency of the whole United States to the slave
power, were scarcely prepared for the sweeping opinion
of Judge Taney, delivered in twenty pages of false
argument, and concurred in by his associates, that
" *black* men have no rights which *white* men are
bound to respect." This decision, if considered and
accepted as such, opened the way for the toleration
of slavery, not only in the territories, but in the free
states of the American Union. It was a bold and
impious attempt to defy the declaration that God hath
made of *one* blood all the nations of men; for this oppressive enactment hinged on the *colour of the skin,*

" *black* men have no rights which *white* men are bound
to respect." Alas! the *white* men have had to learn
by bitter experience that GOD *is no respecter of persons*, and that He himself can plead the cause of the
oppressed, and by terrible things in righteousness can
arise to punish the oppressor and the unjust judge.
This iniquitous decision was useful in arousing a spirit
of resistance in several of the Northern states. New
York, Maine, and Ohio, enacted, that all coloured persons brought by their masters into those states should
be considered free, and there were other bills passed
in reference to the coloured people which indicated a
tendency to righteousness. Of course these bills did
not interfere with the operation of the Fugitive Slave
Law, but Maine decreed that legal defence should be
provided at the state's expense for any person within
its borders claimed as a fugitive slave. Ohio prohibited the state's prisons being used to detain alleged
fugitive slaves; and Wisconsin forbade the enforce-
ment of penalties against any persons within the state
who might be condemned under the Fugitive Slave
Law. Thus the North showed signs of rebellion
against this wicked and arbitrary decision of the
Supreme Court, but even yet had not the sense to
see and feel its degradation and subserviency to the
tyranny of the South, from which it could not free
itself while bound by the Union and its compromises;
but to the abolitionists these transactions afforded
fresh ground for their conviction, that there was no
hope for the independence and liberty of the North
till the Union should be dissolved.

In 1857 occurred that fearful commercial crisis which
passed over the United States, threatening with ruin
and destitution the mighty merchant princes of the
land, and involving in their fall the whole of the North.
The South did not, to the same extent, share these
trials; their *property* was of a different kind, and they
rejoiced in the idea that the panic at the North would
stay the progress of anti-slavery agitation and interference. Not so, however. The cause of the slave
was in the hands of the Almighty, and the voice of all
those warnings calling to repentance was *His* voice.
Some sense of this appeared to visit the nation in the
following year, when a great revival spread over it,
and a time of softening influence was vouchsafed to
try once again if repentance had come. But no; the
heart of the people was hardened still more; they
would not let the oppressed go free; other sins were
mentioned with self-reproach; gaming-houses and gin-
shops in some cases were closed for a time; pulpits
and tract societies testified against dancing and various
immoralities, but not one word was heard against
SLAVERY, that overwhelming sin of the nation, which
comprised within it all other sins in deepest, darkest
degree. At the great revival meetings, notices were
put up that no " controverted topics" should be introduced, the meaning of which was well understood to
be that the subject of slavery should not be mentioned.
Separate places were set apart for the coloured " brethren and sisters" who were under the solemn visita-
tions which appeared to have come upon white men
and women. Revival meetings were also held at the

South, but never was one case known of a slaveholder having under this influence done justice to his brethren, and so their hearts they hardened yet again, and would not let the people go; and more terrible things in righteousness were needed before they could be brought to yield to the will of God.

It was in 1858 that the infamous proscription of the free coloured people in Maryland and Virginia was attempted. Their number was estimated at upwards of 70,000, and it was argued that the existence of these people, many of whom were well-doing and self-supporting, respectable and wealthy, within sight of the slaves, rendered that sort of property dissatisfied and insecure. The plan proposed, therefore, was to expel the free coloured people from their homes, by offering to them the alternative of leaving the state for ever, or of being sold to the highest bidder, the price of the sale being paid into the state treasury for the support of the common schools. These schemes were mooted at an earnest convention of slaveholders held at Baltimore, in Maryland; and what makes the matter more noticeable is, that the men who took the most prominent part in the convention were members of churches. On this point the *Northern Independent* gives the following information:—" From Talbot county, among others, was Dr. E. M. Hardcastle, a Presbyterian; Dorchester county, Hon. Jas. A. Stewart, the son of a Methodist, and a large slaveholder both in Maryland and Texas; Samuel Pattison and Dr. Phelps, both prominent laymen in the Methodist Episcopal Church; Judge E. F. Chambers of Kent, one of the

most talented and conspicuous laymen in the Pro-
testant Episcopal Church. *One of the most painful
things connected with the convention was, that the
leading men in it were among the most influential in
the Methodist, Episcopal, and Presbyterian Churches
in that section of the state.* Could a set of professed
atheists have done worse ?"

A second convention was summoned to decide on
the details. This was held in June 1859, and then it
was found that, as the *New York Tribune* well expressed it, "there was a Balaam in Maryland." The
convention had met to blast the coloured people, and
were obliged to confess, from careful calculation, that
they could not afford to do so, as thereby they would
expel their best labourers and artizans; and we have
the important testimony of the slaveholders of Maryland themselves, that the removal of the free coloured
people from the state " would deduct nearly fifty per
cent. from the household and agricultural labour furnished by people of colour, and indispensable to the
people of the state. . . . It would produce great dis-
comfort and inconvenience to the great body of slaveholders, would break up the business and destroy the
property of a large number of landholders and land-
renters, a class whose interests are entitled to as much
consideration as those of any portion of our citizens."
So the convention dispersed, concluding that the general removal of the free blacks from the state of Maryland would be " impolitic, inexpedient, and uncalled
for by any public exigency that could justify it."

The State of Arkansas, however, carried out the

infamous provisions of expelling or enslaving the free
coloured people of that state; and as none preferred
the alternative of becoming slaves, the month of January 1860 saw the steamboats and other conveyances
crowded by numbers of unoffending exiles whose lives,
according to reliable testimony, were well-doing and
orderly, but who had been sent adrift, deprived of
their homesteads and means of livelihood, with property very greatly diminished, merely to satisfy the
fears and prejudices of the slaveholders; and no voice
throughout the Union, save those of the abolitionists,
was raised to utter one word of rebuke of this despotic
villany. The same system prevailed, as we have seen,
with regard to white men whose influence was in the
slightest degree suspected of interfering with the security of slave property. This year formed no exception
to its predecessors in this respect, but added many
names to the list of sufferers from this species of
tyranny.

At the end of the year 1858 occurred the Oberlin
rescue case, to which reference is made in the early
part of this narrative, when thirty-seven respectable
men were lodged in jail and brought to trial, accused
of aiding the escape of a poor slave boy who had been
seized by force and fraud to be returned to slavery. Of
the many noble utterances on this occasion we shall
only give one quotation as an illustration; it is part of
a speech by a coloured man named Langston, and shows
the kindred spirit which actuates those who dedicate
themselves to humanity, whatever be the colour of
their skin. His defence is argued with great skill and

fervour. He describes the state of feeling among the
coloured people in the knowledge that kidnappers were
among them, the fear of mothers in sending their children to school, the conviction they had that there was
no law for their protection, and the intense excitement
that prevailed when on the 13th of September it was
reported that an actual seizure had taken place in the
neighbourhood, and that a poor young man was about
to be carried off by fraud and force from their midst.
He goes on to say,—" Being identified with that man
by race, by colour, by manhood, by sympathies such as
God has implanted in us all, I felt it my duty to go
and do what I could towards liberating him.   I had
been taught by revolutionary fathers that the funda-
mental doctrine of this government was that *all* men
have a right to life and liberty. Deeply impressed with
these sentiments I went to Wellington, and hearing on
what authority the parties held the boy in custody, I
conceived, from the little knowledge I had of law, they
had no right to him. . . . It is said that they had a
warrant. Why then should they not establish its validity before the proper officers? To procure such a
lawful investigation of the authority was almost the
sole part I took in that day's proceedings. I supposed
it to be my duty, as a citizen of Ohio—excuse me for
saying that, sir—as an *outlaw of the United States*, to
do what I could to secure at least this form of justice
to my brother whose liberty was in peril. . . . The
law under which I am arraigned is an unjust one,
made to crush the coloured man, and one that outrages
every feeling of humanity and every rule of right. I

have nothing to do with its constitutionality; about that I care but little. . . . But I have another reason to offer why I should not be sentenced, and one that I think pertinent to the case. I have not had a trial before a jury of my peers." He gives a *resumé* of the common law of England, and of the prejudices which render its application impossible towards a coloured man in the United States. " I was tried by a jury who were prejudiced, before a court that was prejudiced, prosecuted by an officer who was prejudiced, and defended, though ably, by counsel who were prejudiced. And therefore it is, your honour, by all that is great and good in manhood, that I should not be subjected to the pains and penalties of this oppressive law, when I have not been tried by a jury of my peers, or a jury that is impartial.

" One word more, sir, and I have done. I went to Wellington knowing that *coloured men have no rights in the United States which white men are bound to respect;* that the courts had so decided; that Congress had so enacted; that the people had so decreed. . . . I, going to Wellington with the full knowledge of all this, knew that if that man was taken he was hopelessly gone, no matter whether he had been in slavery before or not. I knew that I was in the same situation myself, and that, by the decision of your honour, if any man whatever were to claim me as his slave and seize me, and my brother being a lawyer should seek to get out a writ of *habeas corpus* to expose the falsity of the claim, he would be thrust into prison under one provision of the Fugitive Slave Law, for interfering with a

man claiming to be in pursuit of a fugitive; and I, by
the perjury of a solitary wretch, would by another of
its provisions be helplessly doomed to a life-long bondage, without the possibility of escape. . . .

"But in view of all the facts, I say, that if ever
again a man is seized near me, and is about to be carried southwards as a slave before any legal investigation has been had, I shall hold it to be my duty, as I
held it that day, to secure for him, if possible, a legal
inquiry into the claims by which he is held. And I go
further; I say, that if it is judged illegal to procure
even such an investigation, then we are thrown back
upon those last defences of our rights which cannot be
taken from us, and which God gave us that we need
not be slaves. . . . And now I thank you for this leni-
ency, this indulgence, in giving a man unjustly condemned by a tribunal before which he is declared to
have *no rights* the privilege of speaking in his own
behalf. . . . I shall submit to the penalty, be it what it
may. But I stand up here to say, that if for doing
what I did do on that day at Wellington I am to go to
jail for six months and pay a fine of 1000 dollars, and
if such is the protection the laws of the country afford
me, I must take upon myself the responsibility of self-
protection, when I come to be claimed by some perjured
wretch as his slave. I shall never be taken into slavery.
And as in that trying hour I would have others to do
to me, as I would call on my friends to help me, *so,
help me God*, I stand here to say that I will do all I
can for any man thus seized and held, though the in-
evitable penalty of six months' imprisonment and 1000

dollars for each offence that hangs over me! We have all a common humanity, and you would all do that; your manhood would require it; and, no matter what the laws might be, you would honour yourself for doing it, while your friends and your children to all generations would honour you for doing it, and every good and honest man would say you had done right!"

In April 1859 a very interesting slave case was tried at Philadelphia before Commissioner Longstreth. A coloured man, of the name of Daniel Webster, was arrested on the charge of being the fugitive slave of Mr. Simpson, Virginia. The case for the prisoner was defended with singular ability and legal skill by Messrs. Earle, Hopper, and Pierce, who undertook at an hour's warning the cause of the friendless fugitive. The evidence and incidents and cross examinations were of the most exciting character. The trial commenced on Saturday afternoon, but the prisoner's counsel insisted on an adjournment. On Monday the evidence for the slaveholder proceeded, and then the counsel insisted on a second adjournment, which was granted to four o'clock on Tuesday. The trial proceeded all through the night till six o'clock next morning; then the Commissioner adjourned till the afternoon, when he would give decision. By this time the whole city was in a state of intense excitement, interest, and sympathy; a striking proof of which was, that in some of the revival prayer-meetings the standing order against " controverted topics" was set aside, and the preservation of Daniel was prayed for. In the afternoon the crowded court sat in breathless attention to listen to the deci-

K

sion. The hopes of the abolitionists were very low,
yet they had determined to stand by Daniel to the
last, and contest his case well. The Commissioner
began to sum up the evidence; there was a hard dry-
ness at first which justified the fears of the slave's
friends, then the tone a little changed, and a breathing
of hope was communicated from one to another; then
came the words, " It is not only a question of property
that is at issue, it involves *the liberty or bondage of a
human being*. The case of identity was not proved,
and the prisoner must be discharged." " Thank God"
rose to the hearts and lips of the abolitionists, and the
acclamations of the crowd were most enthusiastic.
The exciting shouts could with difficulty be repressed,
till the final words were pronounced, " I order the
prisoner to be discharged." Then Daniel was carried
off exultingly by his coloured brethren, and conducted
to a place of quiet and safety, while the friends of the
cause felt they had obtained a triumph to cheer them
on their arduous course of duty, and to encourage
them to struggle for the repeal of the odious enactment whereby a man could be tried as a fugitive slave
in Pennsylvania, and the soil of that state made a
hunting-ground for these unoffending outlaws.

CHAPTER X.

KANSAS.—DR. DOY.—JOHN BROWN.

DURING the years 1855–56–57–58, the state of matters in Kansas continued to cause the greatest political agitation in Congress and throughout the United States. Whatever may be said of the struggle *now* going on between the North and South, the struggle in Kansas was *really* one for freedom, and this was the cause of the intense feeling excited respecting it. To detail the various changes and suggested compromises would occupy too much of our space. It is sufficient to say, that after protracted struggle and intense suffering on the part of the free settlers, they were powerful enough in their love of liberty to reject all pro-slavery propositions, and in 1860 Kansas came in as a free state to the Union. The deaths of the heroic settlers in defence of their position, and the sufferings of the women and children from exposure to cold, destitution, anxiety, and terror, entitle them to rank among the martyrs to freedom in the United States. Hitherto Kansas has proved true to its early principles; it has given homes to refugee slaves, repelled all kidnappers, and furnished the most decidedly antislavery brigade of the Northern army.

We may briefly notice the case of Dr. Doy as an illustration of Kansas character. Dr. Doy, his son, and another white man, were conducting thirteen coloured men and women to a place of safety in the interior, as they had been in too perilous proximity to the Missouri

K K

border. All these coloured people were free. They had gone about ten miles, when they were suddenly surprised and surrounded by a band of armed and mounted men, among whom were the mayor and marshal of Weston, and the postmaster of Lawrence. They were commanded to stop, and Dr. Doy was ordered to drive the waggon back to Leavenworth. On his replying that he would never drive any one back to slavery, he was seized and bound, and pistols were held at his head, while the waggons and other property were forcibly driven off through Leavenworth. The prisoners were compelled to enter the boat by guns being pointed at them, and reached Weston before morning. Dr. Doy and his son were held to bail for 5000 dollars, in default of which they were lodged in Platte jail, and there suffered extreme hardship and indignity (which Dr. Doy has detailed in a spirited narrative) for two months. He was then removed to another jail at St. Joseph's, remanded to take his trial on the 20th of June. The trial came on, and he was sentenced to five years' imprisonment, with hard labour. Against this sentence he appealed; but as no justice was to be meted out to him, his friends grew weary, and by a bold stratagem a little band entered the prison at night and led him forth in safety to his home in Kansas. His son and the other white man had been previously released; but the poor coloured people were given up to various persons claiming to be their owners, and became slaves. Such were the doings of the Missouri ruffians in Kansas on behalf of the slave power of the Southern states of America.

On the 2nd of December 1859 the most conspicuous instance of martyrdom to the cause of the slave occurred, when Captain John Brown was executed, for alleged treason, at Charleston in Virginia. Although it is scarcely necessary for us to give any details of this remarkable man's life and character, yet a narrative of anti-slavery sufferers would be incomplete without a slight sketch of the movement which so greatly tended to accelerate the crisis of the struggle between slavery and freedom.

John Brown, a direct lineal descendant of the Pilgrim Fathers, was born at Torringford, Connecticut, on the 9th of May 1800. He seems from very early days to have had an interest in the oppressed coloured people. In 1855 he went to Kansas, when for the sake of freedom it was necessary that that territory should be peopled by free soil emigrants to prevent its entering the Union as a slave state. Here his mills were burned down, his life threatened, and his two sons slain in the most cruel manner. Thenceforth he felt impelled to join in the struggle for freedom in Kansas; and to his determination and bravery it is generally believed should be attributed the ultimate freedom of the state. After this he dedicated his life to the rescue of the suffering bondsmen. On one occasion he passed through Iowa, at a time when a price of 3,000 dollars had been put upon his head by the Governor of Missouri, with twelve or thirteen slaves whom he was escorting from slavery to freedom. He said to a friend at whose house he lodged, " As God spares me, I will deliver the poor that cry ;" and with this determination

strong in his heart, he prepared for an attempt at
rescue on a larger scale. The occasion for the attempt occurred at Harper's Ferry on the night of
the 17th of October 1859. His intention was to run
off a number of slaves from the neighbourhood, and if
necessary to defend their flight by arms, of which he
had provided a large supply; he had with him twenty-
one men, sixteen white and five coloured, and with
this force several plantations were visited, emancipation was proclaimed to the slaves, and the masters were
taken prisoners in order to render the escape of the
slaves more sure. With these prisoners he then retired
to the arsenal and waited many hours. It was said
that he had intended to go off at once with the slaves,
but that pity for the fears of the slaveholders and their
families had induced him to retreat into the arsenal.
This step was fatal: the building was attacked, and a
conflict ensued which terminated in the death or capture of nearly all of these brave twenty-two men.
Two of Brown's sons, Watson and Oliver, and his son-
in-law, were amongst the killed, and he himself was
severely wounded; but his calm courage and straight-
forwardness of speech continued unabated, and he was
able to answer clearly the many questions put to him;
and not one unworthy word, as far as the records go,
was ever heard to escape from him. No time was allowed for wounds to be healed; his trial was hurried
on, and as he was unable to stand, he was brought on
his mattress before the court. It did not require long
for a jury in a slave state to find him guilty, and in
defiance of all efforts to procure delay, the sentence of

death was pronounced on the 31st of October, to take effect on the 2nd of December.

On being asked whether he had anything to say why sentence of death should not be pronounced upon him, he immediately rose from his mattress, and, in a clear, distinct voice, said,—" I have, may it please the Court, a few words to say. In the first place, I deny everything but what I have all along admitted of a design on my part to free slaves. I intended certainly to have made a clean thing of that matter, as I did last winter when I went into Missouri, and there took slaves without the snapping of a gun on either side, moving them through the country, and finally leaving them in Canada. I designed to have done the same thing again on a larger scale. That was all I intended to do. I never intended murder or treason, or the destruction of property, or to excite or incite slaves to rebellion, or to make an insurrection. I have another objection, and that is, that it is unjust that I should suffer such a penalty. Had I interfered in the manner which I admit, and which I admit has been fairly proved—for I admire the truthfulness and candour of the greater portion of the witnesses who have testified in this case—had I so interfered in behalf of the rich, the powerful, the intelligent, the so-called great, or in behalf of any of their friends, either father, mother, brother, sister, wife, or children, or any of that class, and suffered and sacrificed what I have in this interference, it would have been all right, and every man in this Court would have deemed it an act worthy of reward rather than punishment.

" This Court acknowledges too, as I suppose, the
validity of the law of God. I see a book kissed, which
I suppose to be the Bible, or at least the New Testament, which teaches me that all things whatsoever I
would that men should do to me, I should do even so
to them. It teaches me further to remember them
that are in bonds as bound with them. I endeavoured
to act up to that instruction. I say I am yet too
young to understand that God is any respecter of persons. I believe that to have interfered as I have done,
as I have always freely admitted I have done, in behalf of His despised poor, is no wrong, but right.
Now, if it is deemed necessary that I should forfeit
my life for the furtherance of the ends of justice, and
mingle my blood further with the blood of my children and with the blood of millions in this slave
country, whose rights are disregarded by wicked,
cruel, and unjust enactments, I say let it be done.

" Let me say one word further. I feel entirely satisfied with the treatment I have received on my trial.
Considering all the circumstances, it has been more
generous than I expected. But I feel no consciousness of guilt. I have stated from the first what was
my intention, and what was not. I never had any
design against the liberty of any person, nor any disposition to commit treason or excite slaves to rebel or
make any general insurrection. I never encouraged
any man to do so, but always discouraged any idea of
that kind. Let me say also in regard to the state-
ments made by some of those who were connected
with me. I fear it has been stated by some of them

that I have induced them to join me, but the contrary is true. I do not say this to injure them, but as regretting their weakness. Not one but joined me of his own accord, and the greater part at their own expense. A number of them I never saw, and never had a word of conversation with till the day they came to me, and that was for the purpose I have stated. Now, I have done."

He then adjusted his mattress as before, and calmly heard the sentence of death pronounced upon him. The secret of his serenity, and an insight into his remarkable character, are given in letters to several persons which he wrote from prison, and these are so beautiful and admirable, that we would willingly quote from them did space permit. To Mrs. Child, on declining her kind offer to come and nurse him in prison, he says, " I am quite cheerful under all my afflictive circumstances and prospects, having, as I humbly trust, ' the peace of God which passeth all understanding,' to rule in my heart." This was the key-note of the whole. We need scarcely add more, yet at the risk of reiterating familiar things, we cannot refrain from giving his last letter to his family; it contains instruction which may well be accepted by all classes in life.

JOHN BROWN'S LAST LETTER TO HIS FAMILY.

" Charlestown Prison, Nov. 30, 1859.

" My dearly beloved Wife, Sons, and Daughters, every one.— As I now begin what is probably the last letter I shall ever write to any of you, I conclude to write to all at the same time.

" I am waiting the hour of my public murder with great composure of mind and cheerfulness, feeling the strong assurance that in no other possible way could I be used to so much advantage to the cause of God and of humanity, and that nothing that I or all my family have sacrificed and suffered will be lost. The reflection that a wise and merciful, as well as just and holy God, rules not only the affairs of this world, but of all worlds, is a rock to set our feet upon under all circumstances, even those most severely trying ones into which our own feelings and wrongs have placed us.

" Oh! my dear wife and children, would to God you could know how I have been travailing in birth for you all, that no one of you may fail of the grace of God through Jesus Christ; that no one of you may be blind to the truth and glorious light of His Word, in which life and immortality are brought to light. I beseech you, every one, to make the Bible your daily and nightly study, with a child-like, honest, candid, teachable spirit of love and respect for your husband and father. And I beseech the God of my fathers to open all your eyes to the discovery of the truth. You cannot imagine how much you may soon need the consolations of the Christian religion. . . . My dear young children, will you listen to this last poor admonition of one who can only love you ? O! be determined at once to give your whole heart to God, and let nothing shake or alter that resolution. You need have no fears of regretting it. Do not be vain and thoughtless, but sober-minded, and let me entreat you all to love the whole remnant of our once great family. Try and build up again your broken walls, and make the utmost of every stone that is left.

" Nothing can so tend to make life a blessing as the consciousness that your life and example bless others, and leave you the stronger. It is ground of the utmost comfort to my mind to know that so many of you as have had the opportunity have given some proof of their fidelity to the great family of man. Be faithful unto death; from the habitual exercise of love to man, it cannot be very hard to love his Maker. I must yet insert the reason for my firm belief in the inspiration of the Bible, notwithstanding I am perhaps naturally sceptical, certainly not credulous. I wish all to consider it thoroughly when you read that blessed book, and see whether you cannot discover such evidence yourselves. It is the purity of heart filling our minds, as well as work and actions, which is everywhere insisted on, that distinguishes it from all other teachings, that commends it to every conscience.

Whether my heart be willing and obedient or not, the induce-
ment that it holds out is another reason of my convictions of its
truth and genuineness; but I do not here omit my last argument
on the Bible, that eternal life (of which it speaks) is what my
soul is panting after at this moment. I mention this as a reason
for endeavouring to leave a valuable copy of the Bible, to be carefully preserved in remembrance of me, to so many of my posterity,
instead of some other book at equal cost.

" I beseech you all to live in habitual contentment with moderate circumstances and gains of worldly store, and earnestly to
teach this to your children, and children's children after you, by
example as well as by precept.

" Be sure to owe no man anything, but to love one another.
John Rogers wrote to his children, ' Abhor that arrant whore of
Rome;' John Brown writes to his children to abhor, with undy-
ing hatred also, *that sum of all villanies*—SLAVERY.

" Remember, he that is slow to anger is better than the mighty,
and he that ruleth his spirit than he that taketh a city. Remember also, that they being wise shall shine, and they that turn
many to righteousness, as the stars for ever and ever.

" And now, dearly beloved family, to God and the word of his
Grace I commend you all. Your affectionate father,

" JOHN BROWN."

His conduct in prison was in striking consistency
with his character, and he bore faithful testimony
against those who professed to be ministers of the
Gospel and yet sanctioned slavery. On being asked
if he would wish to have the services of a minister on
the day of execution, he said that he desired no religious ceremonies, either in the jail or on the scaffold,
from ministers who consent to or approve of the en-
slavement of their fellow-creatures; that he would
prefer rather to be accompanied to the scaffold by a
dozen slave children and a good old slave-mother,
with their appeal to God for blessings on his soul,
than all the eloquence of the whole clergy of the com-

monwealth combined. On leaving the prison, on the
day of his death, a poor negro woman and her child
stood near him; the old man's eyes softened; he
stooped and kissed the child; and thus, by his last
voluntary act on earth, put the seal to his legacy of
sympathy and love for the oppressed race for whom
he had lived and laboured and died. Almost his last
words were, " I contemplate my death with composure and calmness. It would undoubtedly be pleasant
to live longer; but as it is the will of God that I should
now close my career, I am content. It is doubtless
best that I should be thus legally murdered for the
good of the cause, and I am prepared to submit without a murmur. . . . I can probably serve the slave
better by my death than by my life. . . . I am not a
stranger to the way of salvation by Christ. To me it
is given, in behalf of Christ, not only to believe on
Him, but also to *suffer* for His sake. . . . I think I
feel as happy as Paul did when he lay in prison. . . .
I do rejoice; yea, and will rejoice."

Such was the man whom the United States selected
as the first traitor of the commonwealth; for it is remarkable that his was the first execution for *treason*
the republic had witnessed. Of the nature of his *crime*
(that of seeking to confer liberty on the most oppressed
of human beings), of his sentence, of its justice, the
civilized world forms its judgment now, and posterity
will form a yet sterner judgment hereafter.

Virginia consummated the infamy on the 2nd of
December 1859; and, before two years had rolled
round, the blood of her own sons had crimsoned her

soil, and Harper's Ferry was one of the first contested points of battle between the North and South in their fratricidal war. John Brown's remains were delivered to his widow, and, under the care of sympathising friends, were conveyed through Philadelphia and New York to the home farm at North Elba, where the family were settled, while the father and the sons went to aid the cause of the oppressed. John Brown himself had indicated a great rock on the farm near which he wished to be buried, and, in accordance with this wish, the mournful party, after a journey of fatigue and difficulty, reached North Elba. The meeting between the widowed Marianne Brown and the widowed daughter and daughters-in-law and the fatherless children, may be better conceived than described; but emotion was soon subdued, theirs was not the family to indulge grief too long, and even the little one of five years old became calm, and quietness prevailed, for they, too, belonged to the martyr band. Next day, in the presence of his loving family and faithful friends, by the rock on the farm at the base of the Adirondack mountains, were deposited the mortal remains of this noble man.

Two weeks after, three of his remaining companions were executed at Charleston. Each of the men connected with the Harper's Ferry insurrection would merit particular notice, for it is remarkable that they were all men of no common stamp, and several of them have left letters and testimonies worthy of the associates of John Brown. For these we refer our readers to other sources of information, which are readily

available; and we are well assured they will be interested by further acquaintance with the Harper's
Ferry band.

In commenting upon the departure from the previously arranged plans at Harper's Ferry, the American Anti-Slavery Society's Report says, " It was not
decreed that they should do what they attempted; at
least not in the way they undertook it. They were
too few to break for the slave a path to Freedom
through the hostile array of a slave-holding nation in
arms; but not too few to bear a glorious testimony
before that nation and all nations, that the cause of
impartial Freedom, of justice to the poorest and weak-
est of GOD's children, is a cause worth dying for; and
can inspire souls large enough to comprehend its worth,
with courage to smile at danger, and strength to
triumph over death. And the power of such a testimony who can measure? How far it shall reach, how
long it shall act unexhausted, nay, with still growing
force, who can estimate? It certainly looks strange,
at first view, that one so well fitted as John Brown
had often shown himself for all the exigencies of gue-
rilla warfare, should let slip the favourable moment of
escape from enemies who, he could not have doubted,
would speedily gather round him in overwhelming
numbers. But there's a Divinity that shapes our
ends. The firm believer in a universal Providence,
which lets not a sparrow fall unnoticed, nor leaves
unnumbered one hair of our heads, will readily admit,
as the easiest solution of the seeming mystery, that the
shrewd, sagacious leader, being but the instrument of

One far wiser than himself, had been predestined to a higher use than the success of his military plans could have attained. Nor was he, we may believe, unconscious of this possibility, for, writing from his Virginia prison after sentence of death had been passed upon him, he says, ' Before I began my work at Harper's Ferry, I felt assured that, in the *worst event*, it would certainly *pay;*' and expresses his belief that he should have kept to his own plan, if God's had not been infinitely better."

From the same Report we borrow its conclusion of the narrative of the tragedy.* " The martyr's testimony was sealed, the hero's warfare ended. He had fought a good fight with spiritual, if not with earnal weapons; he had finished his course as grandly as he had begun it bravely and unselfishly; he had kept the faith, the loving faith of Him who came to preach deliverance to the captives; for his crown of righteousness we fear not to trust him to the Lord, the righteous Judge; and even for his earthly fame we wait, with not a shade of doubt, the verdict of posterity."

> " They never fail who nobly die for right;
> God's faithful martyrs cannot suffer loss;
> Their blazing faggots sow the world with light,
> And heaven's gate swings upon their bloody cross." †

* " The Anti-Slavery History of the John Brown year; being the 27th Annual Report of the American Anti-Slavery Society.— New York, 1861."

† A correspondent passing through Harper's Ferry alludes to the significant fact, that in the midst of a mass of ruins John Brown's prison stands untouched; and the United States' troops now march to the tune of a singular refrain, in which the name of John Brown frequently occurs.

CHAPTER XI.

NORTHERN EFFORTS TO PROPITIATE THE SOUTH ALL IN VAIN.—
SOUTHERN ATROCITIES.—REV. DANIEL WORTH.—REV. J. G. FEE.—
NORTHERN SENTIMENT RIPENS TO ACTION. — ELECTION OF PRE-
SIDENT LINCOLN. — SECESSION. — CORNER-STONE OF THE SLAVE-
HOLDING REPUBLIC.—WAR.— ANTI-SLAVERY MEASURES OF THE
GOVERNMENT.—CARE OF THE FREEDMEN.

THE judicial murder of old John Brown was charge-
able, not on the South only, but on the whole of the
United States. The North did her best to shake off
the imputation of too great sympathy with him—she
aided the surrender of all suspected of implication in
his attempt, and furnished witnesses to procure their
condemnation. But all this time-serving policy was of
no avail; the indignation of the South, its revenge,
and perhaps its fears, were manifested in the violent
outrages perpetrated on all who in the slightest degree
were associated with the North, and a perfect reign of
terror existed. During the year 1860 no fewer than
723 Northerners were treated with brutal violence at
the South. Between forty and fifty of these were
murdered, many were tarred and feathered or cruelly
whipped, and still more were robbed of their money
and clothing. No local authority interfered for their
protection; on the contrary, the sanction of the most
influential citizens and officials was given to these
outrages. These victims were not even abolitionists;
many of them were teachers, often young ladies from
the North, who had resided many years in the South,
respectably earning their bread; they were summarily

dismissed, and excellent citizens were compelled to leave their homes and fly for their lives, simply because they were originally from the North. Some of them were mere travellers on business, Scotch, English, or Irish, but that did not protect them; they hailed from the North, and consequently they deserved to be sacrificed, to atone for the attempt of old John Brown to run off Virginian slaves. We do not mention these cases as those of victims to the anti-slavery cause, because most of them had no particular interest in it; we simply recur to these atrocities, to show the state of Southern feeling, and the aggravated insults to which the North submitted without remonstrance. But there were two cases at this time to which we may more particularly allude, because they pertain to the narrative of martyrs to the cause. Daniel Worth, a preacher of the Wesleyan Methodist Church, was arrested and thrown into prison on the charge of circulating " Helper's Impending Crisis " (a statistical analysis of the comparative productiveness of slavery and freedom), and of preaching in such a way as " to make slaves and free negroes dissatisfied with their condition." After remaining in a prison cell, wholly unsuitable for any person to live in, during the whole winter, he was tried and condemned to imprisonment for one year. Many clamours were made to have public whipping added to the sentence, but this happily was not inflicted. A correspondent of the New York *Tribune*, writing of him, says, April 7th—" Other trials are impending, and it will be with great difficulty that he will escape whipping. If he does not, he will not

L

146   THE ANTI-SLAVERY CAUSE IN AMERICA

forget that neither did his Master, who came to earth
some centuries ago to preach deliverance to the captives, escape the Roman scourge, and a yet sterner
fate. We do not think, come what may, that he will
desert his Master's cause. He tells us from his prison-
cell, soon after his arrest, and while expecting to endure the utmost rigour of that unjust law, ' I seemed
to hear my Saviour's voice asking, " Art thou ready to
suffer for my sake ?" When I came to the point and
could say, " Yes, Lord, I am willing to suffer thy
righteous will in all things," he poured his love into
my soul so boundlessly, that I shouted aloud for joy.
And let me say, that I fully believe, if I am sentenced
to confinement or other punishment, God will glorify
his name by my suffering for him, as much as though I
was at liberty and working in his vineyard.' "

A recent American paper brings us the intelligence
of the death of this " faithful and beloved brother, who
laboured for a time as missionary in North Carolina.
For his fidelity to God and humanity, his plea for those
in bonds, his rebuke of oppression, he suffered persecution and imprisonment, and was finally compelled to
leave the state. The sufferings he endured while in
prison there, no doubt hastened his death. He was a
good man, and has, we trust, entered into rest."

The other case to which we would refer is that of
John G. Fee of Kentucky. He was the leader and
mainspring of a little band of settlers who were preaching an anti-slavery gospel in this slave state. At a
settlement they had called Berea, they had established
a flourishing school; a steam saw-mill had been erected,

and all seemed to promise fair, not only for the settlement, but for the benefit of the neighbouring country.
The slaveholding party being jealous of this flourishing
free-labour colony, a meeting of the " oldest, *most respectable, and law-abiding citizens*" was held, and a
committee of sixty-five, " representing the wealth and
respectability of the country," was appointed to execute
the will of the slaveholders. This committee visited
Berea, and told Mr. Fee that his principles were " opposed to the public peace," and that he and his friends
must leave the state within ten days. They remon-
strated, but in vain; they found they must consent to go, or be forced away; they chose the former,
and it may be well conceived that this decision involved very severe conflicts and suffering in thus
abandoning the scene of their labours and successes for
so many years. Little offshoots of this Christian band
had settled in other parts of the state, and they too
were visited by committees of the slaveholders, who
desired to be left alone with their darling institution,
and so ordered that these people should all leave the
state by the 4th day of February, which, after taking
earnest counsel together, they resolved to do, and
reached Cincinnati a short time before the day named.
Yet this quiet submission was not enough for the tyrants of the South; they burned or otherwise destroyed
much of the property of the refugees, and visited with
summary vengeance all who seemed to sympathise with
them. The men who were thus expelled from Kentucky were of unimpeachable character, as even their
enemies admitted, and one slaveholder acknowledged

that the neighbourhood thus broken up " was the best in all Kentucky." Nevertheless, they were expelled at the instance of the slave power, and the North made no remonstrance on behalf of the citizens thus ignominiously treated. On the contrary, it did everything in its power to propitiate the South, and to allay the irritation that prevailed there against the North; among other expedients, the rendition of fugitive slaves was zealously prosecuted. This was the course of the men in power, and the party who were the most heard; but the lawlessness of the South was working in another way, soon to manifest itself.

Before passing from the sufferings that have been endured in the South for the cause of the slave, we must not omit to allude to a class which we have no doubt has prevailed to a large extent, a few illustrations of which have from time to time reached us. They are those of slaveholders who have become unhappy in their position, whose consciences have not been too much seared by habit to prevent their feeling the guilt and misery inseparable from slavery. Some of these have with self-sacrificing determination and bravery emancipated their slaves, thus relinquishing all their patrimony, and incurring great expense and danger in removing them to freedom and safety. Of this class we have already mentioned Sarah and Angelina Grimké and James G. Birney, and more recently we have become acquainted with Miss M. Griffith of Kentucky, whose sole inheritance was in slaves. An orphan, she was brought up by a slave " mammy," and in her childhood became acquainted with their agonies and distresses and their yearnings for freedom; her sympathies were all with them, and she determined that when she became of age she would emancipate them all. This she did, and the scene was a most touching one. As she announced to them in turn that they were free, their joy and thankfulness and anxiety for her were beautiful, and she wrote to Mrs. Child on the occasion, " I shall go forth into the world penniless, but I shall work with a light heart, and, best of all, I shall live with an easy conscience." This young lady has not been without anxiety and poverty, but she has never for a moment regretted the sacrifice she made for conscience and right. When about eighteen years of age she published a thrilling narrative from her own knowledge of the workings of slavery, under the title of " The Autobiography of a Female Slave." This brought on her much persecution from her relatives, but it drew attention to the subject in a very faithful and powerful manner.

There are many, whose names are unrecorded, who have given up their worldly position and renounced their so-called property in slaves at the call of conscience, whose circumstances only come to light occasionally and incidentally; one of these we give from the private information of an English lady travelling in Indiana. She remarked, when the whole family assembled for evening worship in the house at which she was staying, that among the farm-servants there came a man of superior appearance, but with a countenance so marred with traces of care and anxiety as to attract observation. On inquiring the history of this man, she found that it was an interesting one. He had inherited slaves from his father, but the possession was to him only a sore trial; his conscience would not allow him to retain them as slaves for his own use, or to appropriate their earnings: to sell them or give them away was equally at variance with the dictates of the silent monitor, and he had no money with which to remove them to a free state. He could not emancipate them, because, by the laws of his own state, they would be at once seized and become liable to be sold into far worse hands than his. The thoughts and anxieties respecting what he should do cost him sleepless nights and agonizing days, and furrowed his face with the traces that will go with him to the grave. He had no friend with whom he dared to take counsel, and his little property wasted away. Providentially at this juncture some members of the Society of Friends travelled that way; he found he might safely consult with them in his difficulties; they spoke cheering and encouraging words to him, which helped him to bear his burden a little longer. On their return home they interested those around them and were enabled to remit to the poor slaveholder the money necessary for his journey with his servants to a free state. There he emancipated them by law, located them on little plots, and left them to provide for themselves, while he took a situation as farm-servant with the family in which our friend saw him. Such a case needs no comment from us to commend it to the admiration of all who read it.

There is another class who have remained, and indeed

who still remain, ostensibly in the position of slave-holders, waiting for means and opportunity to emancipate legally. Their anxiety respecting those in their care, whom they now regard not as slaves but as members of their families, and the difficulties they have encountered in securing safety and freedom for them, owing to the jealous vigilance of those around—entitle them to much sympathy as sufferers in the cause. In the excitement now prevailing in America, we hope a way of escape will be opened for them too.

We have marked the progress of anti-slavery sentiment at the North, which, though very slow and often vacillating, had yet gained the point of banding together a political party pledged to the *non-extension of slavery to the Territories of the United States*. With slavery as it existed in the Southern states it sought not to meddle; but the truth had begun to gain strength, that it would be inexpedient to spread this system of corruption and iniquity into the Territories yet unorganised. The " irrepressible conflict " was still being waged in the Congress and everywhere, and the public excitement rapidly increased till the period came for the presidential election, which resulted in the choice of Abraham Lincoln as President of the United States, a man who had not previously been recognised as an abolitionist, who had pledged himself to non-interference with slavery, and to the support of the Fugitive Slave Law, which he volunteered to make more stringent if it did not accomplish its work with sufficient despatch and certainty. In such a man abolitionists did not place implicit confidence, and the only point

gained by his election was that the North was resolved
slavery should not be extended beyond its present
limits—a very important point, and one which was
felt to be so at the North as well as at the South.
This first decided anti-slavery step of the North could
not be endured. They who had controlled, on behalf
of their beloved institution of slavery, the whole of
the legislation of the United States for eighty years,
could not brook even this resistance on the part of the
hitherto submissive North, and took immediate steps
to withdraw from the Union. So, when they had
made preparation by seizing quietly on many of the
forts and arsenals of the United States, South Carolina
first, and then the other slaveholding states, with the
exception of five, seceded, and formed themselves into
a Southern Confederacy, whose chief corner-stone was
slavery, and its ruling policy the extension, promotion,
and perpetuation of this horrible system. No *other*
motive was ever assigned for the secession; but *this*
was boldly avowed. At the risk of repeating what
must be familiar to most of our readers, we deem it
important to quote the words of the leaders of the
secession, that there may be no mistake on this point.
A. H. Stephens, who is the actual vice-president of the
slave-holders' Confederacy, says, " Last, not least, the
new constitution has put at rest for ever all the agi-
tating questions relating to our peculiar institution—
African slavery as it exists among us, the proper status
of the negro in our form of civilization. This was the
immediate cause of the late rupture and present revolution." Alluding to the ideas of equality of the human

race which pervaded the minds of the founders of the
Republic, he adds, " Those ideas were fundamentally
wrong. Our new Government is founded upon exactly
the opposite ideas. Its foundation is laid, its corner-
stone rests upon the great truth, that the negro is not
equal to the white man; that slavery, subordination to
the superior race, is his natural and moral condition.
This, our new government, is the first in the history of
the world based upon this great physical, philosophical,
and moral truth." He goes on with his arguments:
" It is the first government ever instituted upon principles in strict conformity to nature and the ordination
of Providence in furnishing the material of human society. The substratum of our society is made of the
material fitted by nature for it; and by experience we
know that it is best, not only for the superior, but for
the inferior race, that it should be so. It is, indeed, in
conformity with the Creator. It is not safe for us to
inquire into the wisdom of his ordinances, or to question them. For his own purposes he has made one race
to differ from another, as one star differeth from another
in glory. The great objects of humanity are best attained when conformed to his laws and decrees in the
formation of government, as well as in all things else.
Our Confederacy is founded on a strict conformity with
those laws. This stone, which was rejected by the first
builders, has become the chief stone of the corner in
our new edifice. It is the Lord's doings, and marvellous
in our eyes." We doubt whether, for unmitigated
blasphemy, this concluding paragraph can be matched.
These sentiments were entirely concurred in by the

other leaders of the secession. Senator Tombs and the
president, Jefferson Davis, spoke in equally clear terms
respecting the ground of separation and the grievance
that led to the hostile disruption of the states, viz., the
interference with the slaveholders' right to extend and
perpetuate slavery in the Territories.

Such, then, was the position of affairs when President Lincoln came into office on the 4th of March 1861.
He adopted the most conciliatory course towards the
slaveholding states, trying to win them back by all the
concessions in his power, save one : he was true to the
party and platform which he went to Congress to re-
present, he would not yield one inch on the important
point of non-extension of slavery to the Territories.
Twice was the offer made by the South to return to
the Union if this point were conceded to them; but to
the honour of the President, he was faithful to the
distinctive peculiarity of his party. He had not yet
been able to see that his best policy was to do justice
to the slave, and that the righteous judgments of the
Most High were impending over his guilty nation because of its iniquity, and that a little breathing space
was still granted for repentance before even the death
of the first-born came as a sad and solemn warning for
North as well as South, to " let the people go." But
this pause was not improved, and at Fort-Sumter the
first gun was fired and the first blood was shed in the
fearful fratricidal war which has come in judgment
for the iniquity of the nation. Then North and South
armed for the conflict. Thousands—tens, hundreds of
thousands of brave youths, the pride of their families,

cheerfully laid down their lives, as they thought, for
their country. Some of them fought for freedom, no
doubt, but the nation generally had no issue of freedom
in the beginning of the strife. The South, after all the
concessions made to her, had provoked the contest, and
the Northern spirit of resistance was at length aroused,
and it seemed as if no end could be seen for the horrible war. Again and again was the President urged to
proclaim emancipation, if not as a measure of justice, at
least as a measure of self-preservation; for, argued the
faithful abolitionists, it is not by force of arms, but by
measures of righteousness, that we can hope for the
favour of the Almighty. The President was tied to his
constitutional oath, and deemed himself thereby restricted from any measure of general emancipation.
Gradually he began to learn what the constitution
would admit, and he acted accordingly : and whatever
we may say regarding his proclamation and its motive,
his other measures, though perhaps promoted by a
general advance in public opinion, seemed to spring
from his " own personal wish that all men everywhere
should be free." He called for a convention of the five
slaveholding states that still adhered to the Union,
and proposed to them a system of emancipation, with
a certain amount of compensation for difficulties that
might be involved in the change of circumstances.
This proposition has been accepted by Missouri, and it
is hoped that very shortly the 26,000 slaves in that
state will become free men; Kentucky, Delaware, and
Maryland have not as yet acceded to these propositions; but the District of Columbia, over which the

Congress has exclusive jurisdiction, is now free, and
compensation from the national treasury is to be paid
to the slaveholders. We hope that in these plans of
compensation, the *rightful* owner will not be over-
looked. For surely Justice says, with Emerson,—

> " Pay ransom to the owner,
>   And fill the bag to the brim.
> Who is the owner ?   The slave is owner,
>   And ever was. *Pay him.*"

We earnestly trust the time for compensation is not
yet past; that of retribution has been, is now, and probably will continue for many days, in a sorrow and
agony which bear some resemblance to the sorrow and
agony the slave has known for generations.

The President by Act of Congress has decreed slavery to be for ever prohibited in the Territories of the
United States. He has forbidden, on pain of dismissal
from the service, any officer or soldier to return fugitive
slaves. He has entered into a treaty with Great Britain
to allow the right of search in African slave-traders,
which former governments had always resisted, and
he has acknowledged the negro republics of Hayti and
Liberia. Then he discovered the war power of the constitution, whereby, although he could not touch slavery
in the loyal states, he had authority as commander-in-
chief of the army to deal with it as it seemed best to
him in those states which had taken up arms against
the Union, and were therefore outside of its protection.
So he issued a proclamation of emancipation, which
took effect on the 1st January 1863, to the 3,000,000
of slaves in the rebel states, inviting the slaves to his

protection, and even to enter his army. All these governmental edicts, it must be admitted, are great strides towards emancipation; and one step taken in the right direction, whatever be the motive, is sure to lead on to another, as the eyes are gradually opened to see the right way; so let us hope for the Northern states that they will go on in the path of righteousness towards the great national deliverance from bondage, a deliverance, not only for the 4,000,000 of slaves, but for the white men and women who have voluntarily bowed down to the yoke of Slavery.

There is another feature in the course of the American Government which has been to us more encouraging than any we have yet mentioned. We allude to the care extended towards the fugitive or deserted slaves who claimed the protection of the Northern troops, believing that there they would find safety and freedom ; and with comparatively few exceptions, they have not been disappointed. About 200,000 of these people are now free and under the protection of the Government, which, considering the present national distress and the crippled state of the national finances, has been very creditably afforded them. Commissioners have been appointed to see that care and instruction are extended to them, and that they be introduced to the system of working under the new regulations. Rations have been provided, and, as far as possible, wages have been paid for work performed in the camp and on the plantations lately deserted by the slaveholders. There is necessarily much distress in some of the colonies of these freed men, who have flocked in by hundreds, in some places where arrangements to provide them work, food, and care had not yet been organized; but in South Carolina, on the islands where the beautiful sea-island cotton is raised, they have been set to work, and thus the experiment of free labour immediately following slavery has been tried, and though under many difficulties, has been completely successful. From Kansas also, where there is more room for their employment, the reports are most satisfactory, and from all the settlements within the lines of the United States armies we learn that the conduct of the freed men and women has been most encouraging, and highly creditable to those who are so often reputed to be unfit for freedom.

We must not omit to mention, among those who have sacrificed to the cause of the slave, the noble men and women, to the number of one hundred and fifty at least, who have volunteered to leave their comfortable homes in the North, the refinement of educated society, and the enjoyment of every luxury, to take the post of superintendents and teachers of those refugees who have been kept as far as possible in heathen darkness by their masters, lest light and then liberty should enter their domains, so dark and full of cruelty. In speaking of this devoted band, the United States Commissioner says :—" It would not be easy again to combine in a body of men so much worth and capacity; and it is but a deserved tribute to say, that but for their unusual zeal and devotion under many adverse influences, added to the intrinsic difficulty of the work itself, this enterprise, on which patriotism and humanity had rested their faith, might have failed of the complete success which has hitherto attended it." One spirited and accomplished woman, along with her son, undertook the management of one of the islands, in which they two were the only white persons in a community of about 350 freed negroes, and the narrative of the incidents of their work, their difficulties, and successes, is very interesting. Such are they who are seeking to compensate the slave, by the only method at present in their power, for the Northern share in the wrongs which slavery has heaped upon them. Are not they worthy to be thought of among the martyr band? and will not our readers remember them with grateful affection for their work's sake, and grant them their aid, if it may be; and, at all events, their sympathy and prayers?

CHAPTER XII.

CONCLUSION.

SUCH is the state of the question of Slavery in America in this year of our Lord 1863. Eleven of the slave states are fighting with desperation for the right to perpetuate and propagate the sum of all villanies; the Northern states are not yet wholly fighting in the name of liberty, but liberty advances; slavery is abolished in the District of Columbia and prohibited in the vast Territories of the United States; four slaveholding states are still attached to the Union, and the largest of these offers to free her 26,000 slaves and to accept the President's offer of compensation for losses by the change of system; a proclamation of the President is issued, offering emancipation and protection to 3,000,000 of slaves in the rebel states, the Government having previously extended care and granted freedom to 200,000 fugitives from slavery, and to all who had in any way served the United States' Government or armies; and the United States Attorney-General has declared the coloured people citizens of the United States, thereby virtually annulling the infamous Dred Scott decision, and showing that justice is beginning to be heard in America; that a purer air is breathed in the North since the withdrawal of the " dead body" of sin which they had so long cherished.

And at this juncture, what is the duty of Britain? Surely it is to preserve strict neutrality between North and South in their contest, and to *proclaim herself on the side of the slave*, as becomes her national hereditary character. Surely, above all, it is the duty of Britain to refuse the right hand of political recognition and national friendship to a Confederacy avowedly, unblushingly, adopting for its corner-stone a system which degrades man to the level of merchandise, which has no respect for the virtue of woman, which robs the cradle, and denies the light of the Gospel to millions of immortal beings. The powers of darkness may be permitted to prevail for a season; but never let Britain be found arraying herself on their side, to her own degradation, and to the injury of freedom throughout the world.

And now, before closing this imperfect narrative, we must return once more to the abolitionists, whose agency in bringing about the changes to which we have adverted even their enemies confess. We have seen the first small ripplings on the dull surface of pro-slavery apathy; we have noted the voice heard from the prison at Baltimore and the small upper room in Boston; we have watched the tide of persecution which could not annihilate its victims, but which rather gathered together bands of earnest helpers to swell the anti-slavery army which spread itself through the whole of the North, and whose influence was felt throughout the Union; we have observed the tone of firm faith and prophetic hope which led them on through all their difficulties, trials, and fiery persecutions, even to the martyr's grave, and the far-seeing wisdom which guided their course of action. It is interesting to revive a few sentences from their published documents of

M

twelve years ago, to show how truly they anticipated the present state of things, and the agencies that should produce it. In 1851 and 1852 they describe the course they had advisedly pursued as the one by which all revolutions have been brought about. " The change first takes place in the ideas of a nation, and the revolution is but the projection of that change into the outer world. All institutions are but the external manifestations of the thoughts of the people maintaining them. The abolition of slavery pre-supposes a revolution. It will be a revolution, for it will radically overthrow and reconstruct the institutions of the nation. It may be a revolution fought out on Marston Moors or Bunker Hills, or its victories may be won on the logomachic fields of parliamentary debate. But come in what shape it may, it will be a revolution. When it will come is hidden from our eyes, but we have faith in the signs that tell that it is at hand.

" There is no reason why our institutions should not be made anew on that republican image, the form of which they now disgrace. And it must, and it will be done; if not by this generation, by a better yet to come. But we verily believe that some be now alive that will see the coming of that day. To hasten the coming of that day is the glorious privilege of the American abolitionist. He is the true conservative and the true reformer. He would destroy nothing in politics or religion that is not perverted to the base uses of the tyranny that broods over the land. He would make republicanism a reality, and restore Christianity from the standard of Moses Stuart and Orville

Dewey to that of Jesus Christ." Such was their view of the work to which they had been called; and when the dissolution of the Union really came, they who had been willing to *endure* all things were also ready to *hope* all things; they saw that the end of slavery drew nigh, and they might too easily give credit for anti-slavery principles to the new agency that had been called to the work; nevertheless, they did not lay down their arms, but determined to labour on " till slavery or their natural lives should cease." The Philadelphia Female Anti-Slavery Society describes their position so well that we give their own words :—" The success that has been granted to thirty years of anti-slavery labour we receive with devout thanksgiving. It is true that our hopes of leading the slave peacefully out of his house of bondage have been disappointed; but the death-blow of slavery has been struck, and the providence of God is leading the slave by another path to freedom. The efforts which failed to bring the whole nation up to the high moral plane on which it could inaugurate peaceful emancipation, have succeeded in bringing a portion of it up to the point whence it would resist the further aggressions of slavery. That resistance has evoked a war which is fast intensifying a sentiment in the Northern heart which will ultimately demand the utter destruction of slavery; and thus, by other weapons than those which the anti-slavery societies of this land have wielded, by another warfare than that which they have waged, their work seems about to be finished.

" We commence another year cheered by the bright

M M

vision of final victory looming up in the near future.
Should that vision recede as we approach, leading us
through years of toil ere we overtake it, the faith
which has hitherto guided our enterprise will sustain
us even unto the end. The tremulous joy with which
the abolitionist anticipates the first notes of the jubilee
song, which he almost hears, will not unnerve his arm
for longer conflict, should it be demanded of him.
Though our hope should be deferred and our eyes not
see this salvation, we know that it will dawn in splen-
dour on the world when the ' Lord executeth righteousness and judgment for all that are oppressed.' This
day of our country's terrible trial is not wholly dark to
us. Through its darkness gleams a hope that soon this
nation laden with iniquity may yet, through the stern
discipline of bloody conflict and mortal anguish, of desolated homes and broken hearts, be taught the lessons
it would not learn from gentler teachers; and, in shame
and sorrow, breaking the fetters it had fastened on its
brother, find itself free to ascend the path to true national greatness."

At the recent Annual Meeting of the American Anti-
Slavery Society, held at New York in May 1863,
the members rejoiced over past successes, and evinced
their united purpose never to give up the conflict till
liberty is proclaimed " throughout all the land, to all
the inhabitants thereof." They adjourned, to meet
again on the 3d day of December next, in Philadelphia, to " celebrate in an appropriate manner the
30th, and they would fain hope, the final Anniversary
of the Society's formation. It was at Philadelphia, in

December 1833, that the noble Declaration of Sentiments, the basis of the American Anti-Slavery Society,
was signed and issued. We give one or two of its
concluding sentences, so that at one glance we may see
the whole bow that spans the thirty years, the primary
constituents of which are faith, hope, and trust in God.
" With entire confidence in the over-ruling justice of
God, we plant ourselves upon the Declaration of Independence, and the truths of Divine Revelation, as upon
the Everlasting Rock. . . . Our trust for victory is
solely in God. We may be personally defeated, but our
principles never! Truth, justice, reason, humanity,
must and will gloriously triumph." At the recent meeting, in announcing the adjournment to December 1863,
W. L. Garrison alluded to the small amount of pecuniary support they had had during the thirty years'
war with slavery, and added, ' Not by might nor by
power'—not by the help of many rich and mighty—
but by the truth and Spirit of God Himself, has the
work been done. God and His government and laws
have been magnified by every success of the Anti-Slavery Cause, and His is the glory of all."

We have thus endeavoured briefly to sketch the
anti-slavery struggle in America and its martyrs, and
we think our readers must be struck by the heroism
and the oneness of spirit which pervaded the band,
and which influence the martyrs to every good and
noble cause, whatever be their country or the special
mission which is given them to uphold.

Some of the sufferers for the American slave have
continued to this day, and we trust they may be per-

mitted to see the end of their labours in his deliver
ance; but some, as we have seen, and many whom we
have not mentioned, have fallen asleep. " They died,"
as Whittier so well says,

> " Their brave hearts breaking slow,
>   But self-forgetful to the last,
> In words of cheer and bugle glow
>   Their breath upon the darkness pass'd."

And we cannot refrain from giving a few touching
characteristic words, in reference to the early labourers
who had passed away, by an illustrious member of the
band. " In those days," said Wendell Phillips, " as
we gathered round their graves, and resolved that the
narrower the circle became we would draw the closer
together, we envied the dead their rest. Men ceased
to slander them in the sanctuary of the grave; and as
we looked forward to the desolate vista of calamity
and toil before us, and thought of the temptations
which beset us on either side from worldly prosperity
which a slight sacrifice of principle might secure, or
social ease so close at hand by only a little turning
aside, we envied the dead the quiet sleep to which we
left them,—the harvest reaped and the seal set beyond
the power of change." (Speech in 1855, at the Anniversary of the Boston Mob of 1835.) And in the
Liberator of the 2nd January 1863, W. L. Garrison
says, in reference to the deaths during the past year—
" This list will suffice to remind the readers of the
Liberator of the loss sustained during the brief period
of twelve months. But the glorious Cause to which
the departed gave their earlier or their later years, in

the face of popular scorn and often of fiery trials, is immortal, invincible, and we trust ere long to be triumphant throughout the land. Its friends and advocates have never been so numerous, its enemies never so broken and dispirited, as at the present time. Whoever may be called away to another sphere of existence, it bears a charmed life, and no weapon raised against it can prosper. Based upon human nature, demanding simple justice for all men, seeking the welfare of the oppressor and the oppressed alike, divorced from all worldly selfishness, inspired by a divine energy, and upheld by an omnipotent arm, it cannot be vanquished though all the hosts of hell assail it, and over it death has no power. Others of the faithful and true are waiting ' to be clothed upon' in God's good time, which may not be far off; but, living or dying, they know in WHOM they have believed, and will remain faithful to the end, ready for every emergency, and through faith overcoming all opposition."

And here let us take our leave, for the present, of these earnest labourers; if, through the illustrations of their mission which we have presented, one prayer has been called forth for the slave, one hearty word of cheer for his faithful friends, one wish to unite in effort for his cause, or one firm determination to resist alliance with his oppressor, we shall feel that we have not written in vain.

We have restricted ourselves, in these brief records, to the sufferings of the anti-slavery workers. We have not ventured to touch on the deeply-exciting narrative of the wrongs of the *slave;* that would carry us far beyond due limits; for never was fiction more thrilling than are the heart-stirring and romantic details with which the true history of the American slave abounds; but we trust it is not needful to present these wrongs afresh in order to induce our readers to bear them on their hearts when permitted to approach the footstool of the God of love and mercy. And let not the abolitionists and their work be forgotten. Let them be continually in remembrance, with earnest desires that they may be preserved through the trials yet in store for them—that they may be found faithful to the end, and that the desire of their hearts may speedily be fulfilled—when they can put off their armour, and sing as did those formerly who witnessed a similar deliverance, " JEHOVAH hath triumphed, His people are free."

THE END.

EDINBURGH :—PRINTED BY H. ARMOUR.

Printed in the United States
By Bookmasters